D1094185

BIGLER'S
CHRONICLE
of The WEST

BIGLER'S CHRONICLE of the WEST

The Conquest of California, Discovery
of Gold, and Mormon Settlement
as Reflected in
Henry William Bigler's Diaries

by ERWIN G. GUDDE

UNIVERSITY OF CALIFORNIA PRESS
BERKELEY AND LOS ANGELES : 1962

University of California Press
Berkeley and Los Angeles, California

Cambridge University Press
London, England

© *1962 by The Regents of the University of California*
Library of Congress Catalog Card Number: 62-17519
Printed in the United States of America

To Dale L. Morgan

FELLOW HISTORIAN OF THE AMERICAN WEST

PREFACE

My first acquaintance with the journals of Henry William Bigler was years ago when I wrote an article about the discovery of gold in California. That was in 1927 or thereabouts. I knew that Bigler had recorded the date of the discovery of the precious metal that became the cornerstone of California's modern development and I wanted to check it. Quite naturally I turned to the manuscript preserved in the Bancroft Library. I discovered to my astonishment that the famous entry, by that time well known to historians, was lacking: "this day some kind of mettle was found in the tail race that looks like goald." The text left no doubt that the discovery was made on Monday, January 24, 1848. But that this entry was not in the manuscript of the Bancroft Library proved that Bigler had not followed verbatim his pocket diaries when he rewrote the story for Hubert Howe Bancroft.

More than thirty years later my friend George R. Stewart called my attention to the Bigler manuscript again. He had perused it thoroughly and told me that it contains information about certain geographical names which I had not treated properly in my *California Place Names*. When I again took up the manuscript I realized what a gem had been in the Bancroft Library for almost a century. At the same time my suspicion was confirmed: the Bancroft journal covering the years 1846–1848 did not represent the original diaries, as had been repeatedly asserted. In fact, in the course of my investigation several different versions of Bigler's diaries came to light, most of them in his own hand. But the original pocket diaries for the years 1846–1848 were not among them.

My first intention was just to edit the Bigler journals for 1846 to 1848 with such additions in footnotes as the variations in the different versions made it necessary. However, I soon felt the necessity of interpolating certain passages to round out and clarify the picture.

It was very tempting to transcribe the journals exactly as Bigler had written them for Bancroft. Contrary to our standard dictionary orthography, he forms the past tense of regular verbs by adding a "t," campt instead of camped; the noun women is incorrectly but more phonetically spelled wimen, the verb might is mite, and for chicken he uses the delightful Virginian chicking. Unfortunately Bigler was not always consistent, and some of his spelling might be misleading; hence I have standardized it in accordance with the now generally accepted orthography of American English. Also many names which Bigler misspells have been brought into their proper established form. Otherwise Bigler's quaint and naturally somewhat old-fashioned literary style has been maintained.

Since I expect this to be the last of a number of journals and reminiscences of Western American pioneers which I have edited and published, and since all my books are intended to be of help to the historian as well as entertaining reading for the educated American, I believe it is not out of place to add a note concerning my principles of "editing." It stands to reason that the opinions of readers differ greatly in this respect. A historian in the same field might smile at the explanation and elaboration of certain names or passages, while a layman who just reads for pleasure or entertainment may be vexed because he is forced to consult other books or skip certain things for lack of background. Hence the principles of editors differ vastly. I have seen editions in which the critical and editorial apparatus simply overpowers the text itself, or in which editors thought it necessary to include all their knowledge of the subject. On the other hand there are editions where not even obvious misspellings of names are corrected and the reader has to find out everything by himself. I have endeavored to make a compromise between these extremes. The educated reader will find an explanation for everything that is not obvious, or references to sources where he may find additional or fuller explanations if necessary.

With gratitude I acknowledge the manifold assistance I have received in the preparation of this book. Elisabeth K. Gudde is the coauthor or coeditor of this as of all my publications. George R. Stewart and Dale L. Morgan, two writers more versed in Western United States history than I, never failed to answer my inquiries. In the Bancroft Library where the book was composed, I had the help of the entire staff, particularly George P. Hammond, John Barr Tompkins, Robert H. Becker, Julia Macleod. Haydée Noya and Leslie E. Bliss of the Huntington Library, Juanita Brooks of the Library of the Utah State Historical Society, Earl Olson, Librarian in the Latter-day Saints Church Historian's Office, Allan R. Ottley of the California State Library, Fritz Kramer of the University of Oregon, Sheila Dowd and the staff of the Map Division, and Isabel Jackson and Elinor Alexander of the Documents Division, University of California Library, Elliot A. P. Evans and Helen S. Giffen of the Society of California Pioneers, Henry Karpenstein, Hazel A. Bigler, Ethel Mae Buell, my faithful secretary—all contributed in one way or the other. August Frugé and Lucie Dobbie deserve my thanks for good advice and careful supervision in making the book. I hope that not too many short-comings of my own will be discovered in spite of all this help.

Eichenloh, Moraga Woodlands, May 31, 1961.

E.G.G.

CONTENTS

ILLUSTRATIONS

HENRY WILLIAM BIGLER
FROM *Century Illustrated Monthly Magazine* (1891)

INTRODUCTION

Like other Mormons, Henry William Bigler kept pocket diaries sporadically throughout his life. He recorded some events of his younger years, his conversion to the Church of the Latter-day Saints, the march of the Mormon Battalion, his participation in the discovery of gold, his trek to the final settlement of the Mormons in what was to become Utah, his second trip to California for the purpose of digging gold for the Church, his two journeys as a missionary to Hawaii and a few other isolated phases in his life. It was obviously not his intention ever to publish these records.

In 1870 George Frederic Parsons's *The Life and Adventures of James W. Marshall* was published. When Bigler read this account he wrote an article about his own participation in the discovery of gold at Sutter's Mill. It appeared in the San Francisco *Bulletin* of December 31, 1870. This article apparently drew Hubert Howe Bancroft's attention to Bigler's diaries, and when he collected material for his works on the history of the Pacific states, he asked Bigler to contribute the recollections of his "travels and adventures on the Pacific Coast."

Somewhat reluctantly, Bigler obliged, and between May 3, 1872, and August 17, 1872, he wrote a journal for Bancroft, in fourteen installments, based on his pocket diaries. The pocket diaries themselves are apparently lost, except the two fragments mentioned below. As will be seen from

1

the following discussion, the historian John S. Hittell apparently had the complete diaries in his hands about 1886. The loss is regrettable but not very important. Bigler's picture of the two fateful years from 1846 to 1848, as we have it in various versions of his diaries, is clear and well-rounded.

It may well be that now lost fragments of the versions may yet be found, or even that some of Bigler's original pocket diaries may turn up in the hands of descendants of Bigler. I did not consider it essential to spend more time searching for such items. It would only be in the interest of philological completeness, but serve no literary or historical purpose. The versions which I have examined are as follows.

Bancroft Version. This account covers the period from July, 1846, when the Mormon Battalion was organized at Council Bluffs until September, 1848, when Bigler arrived in Salt Lake City. This version forms the main body of the text of this book. It is the only version known to me which is complete. Moreover, it was written in one sitting, so to speak, and at a time when the recorded events were still comparatively fresh in Bigler's mind. Some entries in other versions are more detailed. Such additional information, when important enough, is given in footnotes. Interpolations from other versions in the text would have tended to destroy the harmony and unity of the Bancroft version, which is, from a literary and stylistic point of view, a compact and logical entity. The manuscript is preserved in the Bancroft Library under the title "Diary of a Mormon in California."

Huntington Version. This version must have originated about the same time as the journal written for Bancroft. I have labeled it thus because the larger part is preserved in the Huntington Library in San Marino, where it is designated as "Henry W. Bigler's Journal, Book A." It contains an autobiography and entries from December 31, 1845, to September 15, 1847, from April 10, 1848, to April 23, 1848, and from August 9, 1848, to September 28, 1848. The pages containing entries between these dates are lacking and others are only partly legible. It gives the impression of being a copy of the pocket diaries, but it is too detailed for that, often more detailed than the Bancroft version. It was written into a regular bound record book, foolscap size, with imprinted pagination.

It was impossible for me to establish the exact date of its origin. As mentioned in my footnotes there are some indications that it might have been written even before the Bancroft version. All we know for sure is that it was written before November 20, 1885.

This version suffered the strangest fate of all the copies and rewrites of Bigler's diaries—it was used as a scrapbook, presumably by his family, from which the historian Juanita Brooks succeeded in removing with great effort many of the clippings of recipes, poems, prayers, and the like pasted over the text, and salvaging at least the larger part of the version.

Hittell Version. On November 20, 1885, Bigler was approached by the historian John Shertzer Hittell. In addition to inquiring about several phases of the beginnings of gold mining, Hittell asked Bigler's opinion about a lecture he had given on September 9, 1885, before the Society of California Pioneers. Hittell had given Marshall's date, January 19, 1848, as the day on which gold was found in the tailrace of Sutter's Mill. Bigler corrected this: "This is a mistake of Marshall in his recollection and I would not doubt his saying if it were not for the statement of my journal and it says the discovery was made on the afternoon of Monday January 24th 1848." Hittell's interest was now fully aroused and he remained in touch with the pioneer.

First Hittell published in the April, 1887, issue of the *Overland Monthly* the exact date of the discovery of gold —information which had remained undisclosed for fifteen years in the safe of the H. H. Bancroft Library.

Then in the September issue of the same magazine Hittell published the "Diary of H. W. Bigler in 1847 and 1848." This diary covered Bigler's sojourn in California from January 10, 1847, the day the Mormon Battalion ferried across the Colorado, until July 30, 1848, when the group of Mormons marched into Carson Valley on their trek from Sutter's Fort to Salt Lake. Hittell stated that he based it on Bigler's original pocket diaries, having made a copy of them and having revised them "at Mr. Bigler's request." This copy with Hittell's revision is now in the archives of the Society of California Pioneers and it is identical with the article printed in the September issue. It would appear that Hittell then returned the original pocket diaries, because on October 8, 1890, he requested a photograph of the entry of January 24, 1848. Bigler could not find a photographer and therefore sent the four pages from his diary to have the photograph made in San Francisco. On October 29, 1890, Hittell suggested to the old pioneer that these pages of the famous entry be placed under glass in the hall of the Society of California Pioneers" as one of the most important documents of our State." Bigler agreed with the suggestion and wrote these touching words in a later diary:

"It was like parting with old friends and I said, God bless you my old friends, may you be preserved and yet prove to me or my posterity a blessing."

Ledger Version. When Hittell wrote to the pioneer on October 29, 1890, he presented him with a ledger of 550 pages, 'well bound in calf with a spring back lettered with your name." Bigler received this gift with apparent pleasure, but it was not until eight years later that he copied his diaries into Hittell's ledger. We may assume that he did not feel the necessity because he had at some previous time copied a version of the pocket diaries in a permanent book (the Huntington version). That Bigler decided after all to copy it again in 1898 was probably stimulated by his attendance as an honorary guest at the fiftieth-anniversary celebrations of the discovery of gold held in San Francisco in January, 1898. As a consequence of this recopying of his journals it may be assumed that he or his family considered the former permanent copy (*i.e.*, the Huntington version) no longer important and therefore used it as a scrapbook. This Ledger version, as I designate the diaries copied into the Hittell ledger, is now in the library of the Office of the Church Historian of the Church of Jesus Christ of Latter-day Saints in Salt Lake City. The pages containing the entries from November, 1846, to July, 1853, are cut out. Only the six pages with the entries between April 2 and April 23, 1848 have been saved and are preserved in the Huntington Library.

Utah Version. In 1932 the Utah State Historical Society printed in their *Quarterly*, Vol. V, the "Extracts from the Journal of Henry W. Bigler." A note was added that this version was written "about 1898" by Bigler, and that the original diary was in the Bancroft Library! This "1898 version" follows in general the Bancroft version but differs considerably in detail. The section from April 9 to September 23, 1848, was omitted. At the end of this account the missing part was supplied with credit to the Bancroft Library. This additional section is copied verbatim from the Bancroft version. In other words the 1898 version, which had been in the hands of Adelbert Bigler, the son of the pioneer, was lacking these pages and the Bancroft Library filled the gap. The difference in style is obvious to the reader. The Utah version, as printed in the *Quarterly*, also contains a diary of the period from October 7, 1849, to September 25, 1850, and scattered entries and letters of later date.

Day Book. The "Henry W. Bigler Day Book 1848" seems to be the only extant longer fragment of the original pocket diaries of 1846 to 1848. The first pages were missing from the manuscript when transcribed. It contains the entries from July 22 to September 26, 1848. The entries in the Bancroft version are almost identical. On the other hand the few entries that could be compared to the Hittell version, July 22 to July 31, 1848, are quite different. The "Day Book" was in the possession of Myrtle B. Branson, St. George, Utah, when copied by the Utah Historical Records Survey, 1936, but was not acquired by the Huntington Library with the other Bigler manuscripts.

Utah Fragment. Another part of Bigler's diaries, not an original, was rescued by the Utah Historical Records Survey. It bears the impressive but misleading title: "Copied from the Original Journal of Henry William Bigler to Supplement Parts Copied and Published in the Utah State Historical Society." It does not supplement the Utah Version and is a poor copy of the autobiographical sketch and a few diary entries to April 15, 1846.

Huntington Fragment. Consists of six original pages, numbered 103 to 108, with entries between April 2 and April 23, 1848. They belong to the pages cut from the Ledger version. After the entry of April 23, Bigler writes: "Fifty years and 3 months today has elapsed since the gold was found in the tail race by James Wilson Marshall, it was found on the afternoon of Monday 24th

January 1848." This indicates that Bigler wrote this passage on April 24th, 1898, and the rest of the Ledger version near that date.

The Huntington Library also possesses the diary of his trip to the mines in California 1849–1850, designated as "Journal B"; the "Private Journal" 1853–54; "Book G," a detailed diary from May 14, 1857, to January 15, 1859; a diary from 1877 to 1886; and eight odd books with some diary entries, accounts, genealogical items, and copies of letters. But the originals of the important diaries of 1846, 1847, 1848 are not among them.

Parts of Bigler's diaries, besides the Hittell and Utah versions, have been published repeatedly, especially in Utah newspapers. Some were serialized in the St. George, Utah, *Washington Union* in the late 1890's. The entries in the Bancroft version from July 19, 1847, to July 19, 1848, are printed in Stanley's article on Sutter's Mormons. The first part of the diary of the trip to the gold mines in 1849 is published in Hafen's *Journals of Forty-Niners.*

I.

ANCESTRY AND
YOUTH: 1815-1846

Henry William Bigler was born August 15, 1815, on a farm near Shinnstown, Harrison County, in what is now West Virginia. His father was of old Pennsylvania German stock. The progenitor of the family, Markus Bigler,

had come on the brigantine *Richard and Elizabeth* from
Rotterdam, landing in Philadelphia on September 28th,
1733.[1] He and other Biglers came in the wake of the
Pfälzer (Palatine) immigration, which has contributed a
high percentage of the population of German origin in
the United States. The Hoovers, Hillegasses, Hilgards,
Villards, Eisenhowers are among them. The roots of the
Biglers, to be sure, were in the *Mittelland* of Bern in
Switzerland. Sometime between 1671 and 1711 some of
the Biglers had taken refuge in Germany, a harbor of
religious liberty, at a time when the Calvinists in Switzerland were almost as intolerant of their nonconformists as
the Catholic bishops in Germany were of Protestants. The
Biglers, apparently Mennonites, settled somewhere around
Frankfurt-am-Main, whence they joined the great migration upon the friendly invitation of William Penn.

Some Biglers remained in the old country, and in the
Swiss canton of Bern the name is still common. Among
the contemporary members of the family is Rudolf Bigler,
municipal librarian of Burgdorf, who made valuable con-
tributions to the biography of Johann August Sutter, a
name often mentioned in Henry William Bigler's diaries.[2]
In the United States the Biglers spread from the Atlantic
to the Pacific, and include a governor of Pennsylvania,
1852 to 1855, one of California, 1852 to 1856, and the subject of this book.[3]

Bigler's paternal grandparents, Jacob and Hannah,
were both born in Bucks County in Dutch Pennsylvania.

---

1. His name is usually given as Mark. Since this name does not exist
in German as a given name and since it is spelled Marx in some records
his name was probably Markus.

2. *Burgdorfer Jahrbuch*, 1935.

3. The history of the Bigler family has been told in great detail by
Norman Burns. He obviously used the Ledger version for his account
on Henry William.

His grandfather was "industrious, jovial, fond of a dram, heavy-set, handsome, and a full blooded Dutchman." The grandmother was a mixture of Dutch and Welsh, "tall, slender, red-haired and enterprising." Soon after their marriage about 1779 they settled in Somerset County, and in 1787 they migrated to Harrison County in Virginia, where Henry William's father, likewise called Jacob, was born on June 9, 1793.

On his mother's side Bigler was of English and Welsh extraction. His mother's parents, Basil and Mary Harvey, lived in Montgomery County, Maryland, where Bigler's mother Elisabeth, "Betsy," was born January 10, 1794. She died when her son was only twelve years old; the father later married Sally Ann Cunningham.

Bigler has repeatedly written about his younger years, in fact most of the various copies of his diaries are preceded by autobiographies. These accounts deal mainly with his family, because Bigler, like most Mormons, diligently pursued his genealogy. Since he kept no regular diaries in his early youth and had no family papers, the stories about his ancestors, relatives, and in-laws are sometimes vague and told from hearsay. In his later rewrites, when the Mormon predilection for genealogy exerted a stronger influence upon him and old age dimmed his memory, names and dates concerning his family became even less reliable. In the Ledger Version he changed his German ancestry to that of Holland. The name "Dutch" was generally accepted in the middle of the nineteenth century as a designation for German. But when Bigler wrote the later versions, it had become a mere nickname for Germans, and as a national designation was restricted to the people of the Netherlands.

He grew up in the sparsely settled wilderness of Virginia that is now West Virginia. The Indians of the frontier were not yet pacified, and his grandfather plowed the fields with a rifle attached to the beam of the plow. A farmer's family was more or less self-sufficient. Trade and professional craftmanship were unknown: these people wove their own cloth, built their own shoes, poured their own candles. The making of the year's supply of sugar from the sap of the "sugar tree" was an annual festival around the first of March. The countryside was roamed by deer, turkey, and racoon, and also by bear, wolf, and panther. Wild honey and berries were in profusion and provided a few delicacies. Like his father, young Henry learned early to use the rifle, and when hardly seventeen he killed a bear. He spent many months in the fall and winter hunting and trapping. This experience stood him in good stead in later years.

In spite of the frontier isolation, Shinnstown was advanced enough to have a regular school, run by a Methodist preacher. Bigler learned spelling, reading, writing, and algebra, and he wrote an acceptable English throughout his life. His literary style was doubtless inborn. In view of the realism and vividness with which he recorded the march of the Mormon Battalion one is inclined to call him the Xenophon of this campaign, although he was just a private soldier who wrote not in classical Greek but in grass-root Virginia American.

In 1836 his rustic life was interrupted. He was steered into a career which later made him an active participant in the events that consolidated our nation. A narration of these nine years from 1837 to 1846 is found in Bigler's letter to Bancroft, dated Farmington, May 3, 1872. Bigler's account should be taken as a reflection of the events of the following years in the mind of a prejudiced but by no means fanatical Latter-day Saint. No attempt has been made to check or correct the details. This book is not

concerned with Bigler the Mormon, but with Bigler the
Chronicler. His account follows.

Nothing particular occurred till the summer of 1836,
when two "Mormon" Elders came through the country
preaching. My father purchased a Book of Mormon and
I read it. I also read the Book of Doctrine and Covenants
and became thoroughly convinced the Book of Mormon
was a divine record and Joseph Smith inspired and sent of
God, and in July, '37, I joined the Church.

In June, '38, I went to Far West in Missouri, where
for the first time I beheld the Prophet. I went to work
helping to stock a sawmill. I had not been there long when
rumors were afloat that the Missourians were making
threats to drive us out. On the ensuing 4th of July I met
in company with many thousands of our people to witness
the laying of the corner stone of the Temple; had a
spirited address from one of our Elders, in which he al-
luded to the oppression and mobbing we as a people had
received from time to time since the Church had been organized. In that oration we claimed our constitutional
right as American citizens, but at an election held in
Daviess County in the following August the Missourians
undertook to prevent our people from going to the polls
to vote, when a general knockdown took place and the
ground [was] cleared by our people. From that affair
the word went far and wide that the Mormons were doing
terrible things, and the whole country was up in arms to
drive us out. All kinds of falsehood were raised against
us, and at last an army commanded by General Lucas
came to Far West to drive out the "Mormons."

Just before he reached the city, he sent out a white flag,
which was met by a similar one from our people. When

our flag returned, we learned that Lucas wanted three of our people out of the city before they killed the rest. This, I think, was on the thirtieth day of October '38.

Hostilities were not to commence till next morning, and it was during the next day that we learned that this army was sent out by order of Governor Lilburn W. Boggs. When we learned this fact we surrendered, and they took Joseph and Hyrum Smith and several others prisoners. The Governor's orders were to drive out or exterminate us. These prisoners were taken and tried by court martial, condemned, and sentenced to be shot on the public square in Far West, but General [Colonel Alexander W.] Doniphan swore he would be G—— damned if he would have anything to do with that honor, for he considered it cold-blood murder, and he ordered his brigade to take up their line of march and left. This movement of his prevented the prisoners from being shot, or at least it was thought so. The same afternoon that General Lucas arrived with his army, Cornelius Gilliam arrived with his men from the west and joined Lucas, painted like Indians, and Gilliam himself painted with red spots, calling himself the Delaware chief. While General Lucas was on the march against Far West, they killed one of our brethren by knocking out his brains with the breech of a gun, and at the same time some eighteen or nineteen of our people were killed by a mob party at Hauns Mill, thirty miles from Far West, although they cried for quarter. Among the slain was an old revolutionary soldier by the name of McBride, literally cut to pieces with an old corn cutter.[4] The person who did this brave act was Jacob Rogers. A strong guard was kept around Far West so that we could not go

4. Bigler repeats here an unconfirmed statement found in Mormon historiography, including the official history by B. H. Roberts (I, 482). The old man could hardly have been a veteran of the War of Independence.

in or out for firewood without being in danger of being shot at. The weather was cold and snow on the ground, and many of us suffered. The soldiers seemingly just for sport shot much of our stock—hogs, sheep, and cattle.

In February '39 I went to Quincy, Illinois, where our people were fleeing to and were kindly received by the Illinoians. I went to work for a man in Quincy who was keeping a boarding house, at the rate of twelve dollars per month. A short time afterwards a steamboat stopped at Quincy wharf. The mate wanted to hire a deckhand, offered twenty five dollars per month, and a bargain was struck. I went aboard and acted as watchman. In a few weeks I was taken sick and returned to Quincy, hunted up my relatives, and found my father living near Payson. After regaining my health, I went to work on a farm at thirteen dollars per month till wheat harvest, when I got one dollar per day. In August I was called to take a mission to preach the gospel, having been ordained an Elder. After filling my mission I went to Nauvoo and went to work, sometimes by the day and sometimes by the month. I did considerable work in the stone quarry getting out rock for the temple. In the month of August, 1842, I attended a conference held in Nauvoo, when I was again called to take another mission, and it was while I was out on this mission when I heard of the death of Joseph and Hyrum Smith. I was at that time preaching in Ripley, the county seat of Jackson County, Virginia. This was in the summer of '44. They were shot on the twenty-seventh of June by an armed mob painted black. For particulars of this tragedy I refer to the Book of Doctrine and Covenants, page 334, fourth European edition.[5]

Shortly after this I returned to my Father's, who had

5. Neither this nor the American editions give more than meager "particulars" of the tragedy.

by this time got a snug little farm near Nauvoo and was living on it. I made my home at my Father's, working on the farm till the fall of '45, when the houseburning commenced by mob parties and continued to increase to the extent that we had to pack up and move into Nauvoo. Because "Mormonism" did not die out with the death of the Prophet and Patriarch, as was anticipated, and because our people were one in political matters, all voting one way, it appeared that hatred grew in the breasts of people against us to such a pitch that every kind of falsehood that was calculated to prejudice the mind of the public was raised and resorted to. Finally the Governor of Illinois and other leading men proposed that we, the Latter-day Saints, leave the State and go to Oregon or to California.[6]

On Sunday, the ninth of February '46, I crossed the Mississippi River in company with others of our brethren for the Rocky Mountains, as we sometimes said, or to California. To tell the truth I knew not where we were going, neither did I care much, only that it might be where I and my people could have the liberty to worship Almighty God according to the dictates of our own conscience without being mobbed for it, for I knew of no law that I or my brethren had broken that we should be exiled from our homes or renounce our religion. The reason why we were not permitted to live in either Missouri or Illinois can be given in a nutshell.[7] But to return, we went in to

---

6. The best book for a general background of these years is DeVoto's *The Year of Decision.* Solidly packed and thorough to the point of pedantry, too individualistic to be called objective historiography in Ranke's sense, it is nevertheless the most valuable book on the fateful year of 1846.

7. Neither here nor elsewhere does Bigler explain how the resentment of the American people toward the Mormons could be told in a "nutshell." Here too DeVoto gives the best explanation, though not in a "nutshell" (pp. 81 ff., and *passim*).

camp some six miles from Nauvoo on Sugar Creek, to wait and to organize here. President Brigham Young and the Twelve were organizing companies of tens, of fifties, and of hundreds, and on the first day of March we made the first grand move for the great West, traveling slowly, making roads and bridges, stopping and making settlements by the way, putting in crops for those who would follow after us; also sending out men down the country to trade with the Missourians for provisions and for oxen and milk cows. In the following June we reached Council Bluff on the Missouri River.

When the Mormons moved from Nauvoo with the intention of settling somewhere in the uninhabited and little-explored West, they were a sad lot, held together only by their religion, by their elders, and by the spirit of Brigham Young. They did not know whither they should turn their steps. It was not certain yet whether California and Oregon would be parts of the United States, and even if they had been sure—would they not be exposed to the same persecution as they had been in Missouri and Illinois? In the minds of some of the leaders the idea was dawning which was finally realized—to found their colony somewhere in the less hospitable regions between the Rocky Mountains and the Sierra Nevada. The region of the Great Basin offered the best chances of undisturbed development for years to come.

Then something happened that was to change the future of Mormonism and have a profound influence upon the West. In anticipation of the acquisition of the Oregon Territory south of the forty-ninth parallel, President Polk had recommended the building of a string of forts along the road through South Pass to the Columbia River for the protection of the expected migration. The Mormons saw an opportunity here and hoped to undertake the building of these forts as they moved westward.

On January 26, 1846, President Young commissioned Elder Jesse C. Little, the president of the Saints in the New England states, to proceed to Washington, and try to come to an understanding with the government concerning the movement to the West. Little did not reach Washington until the outbreak of the war with Mexico, and to his astonishment he was informed that President Polk had conceived the idea of using the services of the Latter-day Saints to conquer California. A regiment one thousand strong was to march via Santa Fe to the Pacific coast, another one thousand were to reach California by sailing around Cape Horn. After repeated conferences Elder Little was informed that one battalion of Mormons would suffice and that Colonel Stephen S. Kearny, commander in the West, had been informed of the fact.

Kearny, from his headquarters at Fort Leavenworth, charged James Allen, captain of the First Dragoons to organize and take command of the Mormon Battalion. At the end of June the Mormons were scattered in various camps on the east side of the Missouri in present-day Iowa between Mount Pisgah and Council Bluffs. At the latter point Captain Allen appeared on July 1 and presented the proposal to a council of President Brigham Young and other members of the Twelve in camp.

In the above quoted letter to Bancroft, and with similar words in the Utah and Huntington versions, Bigler describes the arrival of Captain Allen in the Mormon camp.

On the thirtieth, Captain Allen and four others with a baggage wagon rolled into our camp, inquiring for

Brigham Young, and on the following day, July 1st, the camp of the Saints was called together near Elder Taylor's tent. Captain Allen addressed them to the effect that he was instructed by Colonel Kearny, who was instructed by the President of the United States, James K. Polk, to invite the Mormon people to enlist or volunteer into the service of the United States for one year to go against Mexico and take California. He wanted five hundred men to be ready to march in ten days and join Colonel Kearny, who was already on the march from Fort Leavenworth to Santa Fe. President Young replied: "You shall have your battalion, and if it has to be made up of our elders."

Now I would remark that about the time that we were leaving Nauvoo, one of our people went to Washington City to engage shipping supplies around the Horn to California for the Navy, and while there he was interrogated in reference to our people, their loyalty, etc., and they wished to know if he thought our people would respond to any call the Government might make upon them as a people. I have always understood that Mr. Benton of Missouri [8] argued at Washington that the Mormons were disloyal and urged that the Government make a demand on us, in order to prove our loyalty, and if we failed to comply there was a plan to call out the military from Kentucky, Missouri, and other places, to cut us off and put a stop to our people going into the wilderness.

There was considerable resentment in the rank and file of the Mormons. It was not Bigler alone who was insulted that they should fight for a government that had given them little protection against the brutalities of the mob, indeed whose representatives, so it was alleged, had openly

8. Thomas Hart Benton, Frémont's father-in-law.

threatened them with extermination. Moreover, they were to leave their women and children in the Indian territory, without sufficient shelter and scant provisions. But as in all totalitarian organizations, they had to obey orders. The power of Brigham Young as the president of the Latter-day Saints was unchallenged.

History has shown that Brigham Young was right. The "Mormon question," to be sure, continued for decades to be an open wound on the body politic of our democracy, but the willingness to send some five hundred Mormons into the Mexican War, their exemplary behavior, and their activities as pioneers in the West gave the Latter-day Saints the first recognition from fellow Americans.

On April 5, 1848, Brigham Young proudly recorded:

"The enlistment of the Mormon Battalion in the service of the United States though looked upon by many with astonishment and some with fear, has proved a great blessing to this community. It was indeed the temporal salvation of our camp . . . and it has proved a weapon of our defense, a blockade in the way of our worst enemies under which the widows, the poor and the destitute, and in fact all of this people, have been sheltered." [9]

9. Golder, p. 247. *The March of the Mormon Battalion,* a joint venture by Frank A. Golder, Thomas A. Bailey, and J. Lyman Smith, gives the best account and numerous documents. It does not entirely replace Tyler's *A Concise History.*

The story of the march of the Mormon Battalion has not only been told repeatedly, but several diaries of other members have been published. The footnotes of sections ii, iii, and iv, are therefore restricted to bringing out variations in the different versions of Bigler's journals, and to incidental information.

II.

THE MARCH
TO THE
GILA RIVER: 1846

The Battalion was made up of five companies—A, B, C, D, and E—one hundred men in each company. We had the privilege of making our own officers from among our own men. I attached myself to Company B, Jesse D. Hunter, Captain. The battalion was mustered into service July 16, and Captain Allen took command as Colonel; [1] the same day he marched us some six or eight miles to a trading post on the Missouri River kept by some Frenchmen. I think the proprietor's name was Sarpea.[2] Here Colonel Allen issued to his men blankets, provision, camp kettles, knives, forks, plates, spoons, etc. On Tuesday the twenty-first at twelve o'clock the whole battalion took up their line of march for Fort Leavenworth where they arrived August 1, a distance of some two hundred miles or more. The same afternoon of our arrival the Colonel issued tents to the battalion. The weather was extremely warm and many were taken sick. I myself was shaking with the ague and we already buried one of our number by the name of Samuel Boly.[3] On the fourth we drew our arms (muskets).[4]

---

1. Captain James Allen had been promoted to lieutenant colonel when taking over the command of the Battalion. The men did not elect their officers; they were appointed by Brigham Young.
2. Peter A. Sarpy, well-known Indian trader.
3. Samuel Boley of Company B died on the twenty-second.
4. The other versions record that the Battalion drew their clothing

FROM
SANTA FE TO SALT LAKE CITY
VIA SUTTER'S FORT

Humboldt River

Donner Lake
Sept. 6,'47

Humboldt Sink
Aug. 15, '48

Truckee

Sacramento

Carson R.

American

Sutter's Fort
Sept. 14,'47–July 3, '48

Pleasant Valley
Sutter's Mill

San Francisco
Aug. 21,'47

Mokelumne

Stanislaus

Tuolumne

Merced

San Joaquin

Kings

Tulare Lake

Kern

Kern Lake
Aug. 3, '47

Los Angeles
July 15, '47

San Luis Rey

Warner
Jan

San Diego
Jan. 29, '47

0   50   100   150   200
MILES

Fritz Kramer '62

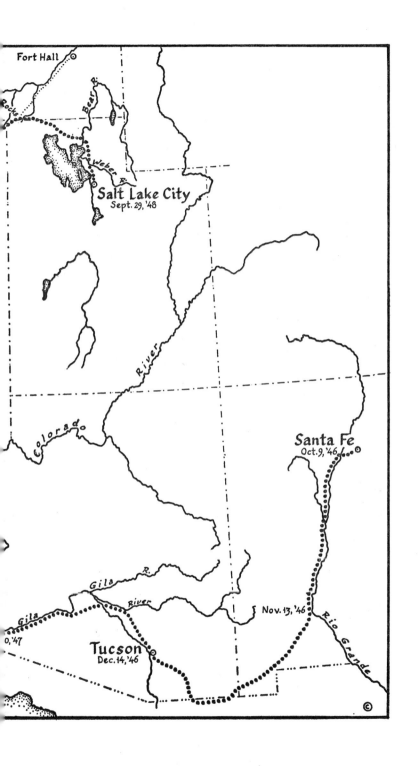

We remained in garrison till the thirteenth, when orders were given to be on the march for Santa Fe. The Colonel remained behind intending to overtake his command in a few days. The weather was still hot and the roads half-leg deep with dust and sand, water scarce, for the brooks and creeks were dry, and it seemed that some of our sick would die for want of water. On the nineteenth, just as we made camp, a storm of wind, hail, and rain from the west was upon us, capsized our tents, upset wagons, and blew some of them several rods into the brush. Hats flew in all directions, and as the hail began to fall every horse and mule put for the timber, leaving their masters to face the storm themselves on an open prairie. This was severe on our sick.[5]

While at this point, our adjutant brought intelligence that the Colonel was sick.[6] On the twenty-sixth our quarter-master (Mr. Gully) [7] arrived from the garrison announcing the sorrowful fact of his death, which occurred Sunday morning, the twenty-third. On the twenty-seventh we arrived at Big John [Spring] or Council Grove,[8] one hundred fifty miles from Fort Leavenworth. Here we halted for a few days as there was plenty of good feed

---

money for the year, $42 each, on the fifth. Most of the money they sent home, but they donated their share to the three Elders who were to leave on their mission to England. In no version does Bigler state that Brigham Young rescued at least part of the soldiers' pay for the Church by sending John D. Lee to collect (John D. Lee, *Journals* p. 9).

5. The Huntington version has daily entries between the twelfth and eighteenth, mostly obliterated.

6. On the twentieth, Captain Hunt baptized the sick people, and in the late afternoon a religious-patriotic meeting was held, with addresses by several officers, which raised the spirits of the Battalion. The next day the whole Battalion prayed for the Colonel's recovery because they "Believed him to be a gentleman" and were afraid a "more tyrannical man" might take command (Huntington).

7. Samuel L. Gully, former third lieutenant of Company E.

8. On the Neosho River. Frequently mentioned stop on the Santa Fe Trail.

22

and a nice stream of water running through the grove.[9]

On the twenty-ninth, the Battalion paid their last respects, which was due their Colonel, James J. Allen, by marching to a shady grove by the side of the creek where a funeral discourse was delivered by Captain Jefferson Hunt of Company A and Adjutant George P. Dykes.

Lieutenant [Andrew Jackson] Smith, being on the march with a detachment of horses under Colonel Kearny, was accepted by our own officers to take command of the Mormon Battalion, he being a graduate of West Point. Notwithstanding that it was the right and the privilege that one of our own officers should have taken the Command, it was thought otherwise, and this honor was conferred on Smith simply because he was a Westpointer.[10]

On the thirtieth, orders were given to be on the march early next morning. That afternoon at three o'clock John Bosco died, and that night by the light of the moon we buried him by the side of his wife (Jane), whom we had buried on the twenty-eighth. As rock was handy, we overlaid and inclosed in one their graves with a stonewall to prevent wild beasts from disturbing them and so stand as a monument to their friends, who may chance to pass that way. Accordingly early the next morning we were on the march, and on the third of September Colonel Smith, as we now called him, began to show his sympathy for the sick by ordering them out of the wagons and swore if they

---

9. The entries in the Huntington and Utah versions from the twenty-third to the end of the month contain only one additional important point. A marginal note added to the twenty-seventh in the Huntington version is characteristic of the suspicion with which Bigler and many others looked upon the military: "I have since understood that there was strong suspicion that the Colonel had been poisoned, fearing perhaps he would be too friendly to the Mormon Battalion."

10. In the Huntington version this entry is placed on the margin between August 31 and September 1.—Andrew J. Smith became a major general in the Civil War.

did not walk, he would tie them to the wagons and drag them.[11]

Now the surgeon who was from Missouri, did not belong to our people, and had been heard to say he did not care a damn whether he killed or cured. Because of this our sick refused to go at sick call and take his medicine. But Smith was told straight up and down, there and then, before we would take Doctor [George W.] Sanderson's medicine, we would leave our bones to bleach on the prairie first.[12]

On the fifteenth we overtook Colonel [Sterling] Price encamped on the bank of the Arkansas River with five hundred horsemen on his way to Santa Fe, where I believe he was to take command of that post. Now it had been Colonel Allen's intention, before we left Fort Leavenworth, to reach Santa Fe by way of Bent's Fort,[13] where he had ordered a lot of supplies for his command, but Colonel Smith had decided he would not go by Bent's Fort, it being too far around. He determined to take a much shorter route, although wood and water were less plentiful. The Battalion being short of grub, and would be more short,

---

11. The Huntington version completes this sentence: "unless they took such medicine as the doctor should prescribe, which they did not like to do." This ties up with the complaint about the doctor in the next paragraph. Dr. Sanderson and his relations with the Battalion are treated in detail by Tyler, pp. 144 ff.—naturally from the Mormon point of view. DeVoto, pp. 325 ff., gives an objective picture of Dr. Sanderson and the sick Battalion boys.

12. The entries from September 4–14 are omitted in the Bancroft version. The entries in the Huntington version contain the usual accounts of the scenery, weather, and lack of firewood. Also a few interesting items. On September 5 Bigler saw the first buffalo, an exciting experience for every traveler. The next day he saw hundreds of them. Several buffaloes were shot and the Battalion enjoyed excellent suppers. At noon of September 11 they reached the Arkansas, of which Bigler gives an enthusiastic description. The buffalo hunt and the arrival at the Arkansas are also recorded in the Utah and Ledger versions.

13. Bent's Fort at the north bank of the Arkansas, about seven miles east of La Junta, Colorado, was in the 1830's and 1840's one of the most important trading centers at a branch of the Santa Fe Trail.

inasmuch as they had now abandoned the idea of going by way of Bent's Fort, the Colonel sent his quartermaster over to Colonel Price's Company about one fourth of a mile to get a little provision. Word was sent back that they did not haul grub for the Mormons. This raised Colonel Smith's Irish a little, and he sent back word and swore if they did not let him have some, he would let loose the Mormons and come down on them with his artillery. This had on Smith's part the desired effect.[14] We remained here two days. Alva Phelps of our Battalion died and was buried at this place.[15]

On the seventeenth while on the march, two buffalo came running parallel with our line, when a whole battalion of balls [bullets] was sent after them. The result was one buffalo got a broken leg and made off to parts unknown. That day we marched twenty-three miles and encamped without wood or water, but there were plenty of buffalo chips, which make an excellent fire in a dry time.[16]

14. This incident is recorded in the Huntington version in similar words. In the Ledger version as well as in the Huntington version, Bigler added: "Colonel Price was in command of a company of mob militia at Far West and sanctioned the shooting of Joseph the Prophet and others on the public square in '38." Colonel Sterling Price was in command of the second Missouri infantry in Kearny's army.

15. "It was believed that Doctor Sanderson's medicine killed him; he gives calomel, and the sick are almost physicked to death" (Utah). Similar complaints are found in the other Mormon diaries. Bigler and all Saints believed in healing a person by "laying hands" on him or by use of botanic medicine.

16. The Huntington version, under date of the seventeenth has a lengthy discussion concerning the successor of the dead Lieutenant Colonel Allen. This phase of the march of the Battalion is fully discussed with documents in Golder, pp. 150–171.

Under the same date the Utah version has a lengthy story that the camp was aroused the preceding night by a star in the east moving up and down and sideways. Although Bigler admits that he "could not see anything of the sort," he nevertheless states that it was about this time when the mob drove out the rest of the Mormons from Nauvoo. Tyler (p. 158), who either had better eyesight or was a better Mormon, saw the dancing star and connected it with Phelps's being "physicked to death."

On the eighteenth, we marched twenty-five miles and encamped without water for our animals and a very scanty supply for the men. That day was very warm; teams gave out and men, too, for want of water. The men who had given out had to be brought to camp in wagons. After we had marched about twenty miles, we came to a small dirty, muddy pond of water, tramped up by the buffalo. The water was well mixed with their green manure and was at a temperature of about ——. The men drank without complaining, but gracious how sick it made some of them.[17]

On the third of October we were met by an express from General Kearny that if the Battalion was not in Santa Fe by the tenth, it would be rejected. In order to be in time, the sick were left with a few to take charge and bring them up, and all the strong and able had to proceed on a forced march for Santa Fe, where they arrived on the ninth, and on the twelfth the rear arrived.

On the thirteenth of October, Lieutenant Colonel Cooke took command of the Battalion by order of General Kearny. Lieutenant A. J. Smith, who had acted as Colonel pro tem on the death of Colonel Allen, was made quartermaster, and our own former quartermaster removed.

Why this was, I never knew.

On the fifteenth orders were given for Captain James Brown of Company C to take a detachment with all the sick and feeble, about one hundred men all told, and go to Pueblo on the Arkansas.[18] On the eighteenth they left for

---

17. The Huntington version has routine entries from the nineteenth to the twenty-sixth, but no further entries until October 9. Bigler explains: "I have not journaled anything since the 26th of September, having traveled since then 257 miles or thereabout."

18. Captain James Brown's and Lieutenant Willis's detachments wintered at Pueblo. In the following spring they were to play a conspicuous role in the westward movement of the Mormons. The corresponding order for the detachment and the list of men comprising it is in Tyler, 166 ff. Captain James Brown was the uncle of the James Brown who

that place, and on the nineteenth Colonel Cook took up his line of march for California. I understood that his pilots, Messrs. Weaver, Charbonneau, and Leroux,[19] advised him to lay in one hundred twenty days of provisions for his command. His reply was he would only lay in sixty because he could not get teams to haul that amount. How that was, I do not know; I know this much that we were soon put upon three-quarter rations and soon after on half rations.

We marched down the Rio Grande about three hundred miles, and on the eleventh of November a detachment of fifty men under Lieutenant [William M.] Willis was sent back to the Pueblo, because the most of them were considered to be too feeble in health to carry their guns and knapsacks through to the Pacific Coast.[20] About this time the cattle the Colonel had for beef became so reduced in flesh that they began to give out by the way, and the soldiers, being on short allowance, would kill one whenever it gave out, dress it, and bring it in to camp and eat it. Mules

---

was present when gold was discovered and who wrote a questionable account of it. See section viii.

19. The chief guide was Pauline Weaver, a former employee of the Hudson's Bay Company and repeatedly mentioned in the employ of United States troops. Antoine Leroux, a French Canadian, was likewise a well-known guide (Bieber, p. 85). Jean Baptiste Charbonneau, who as an infant went to the Pacific and back with Lewis and Clark, was the other mentioned guide, called Shavenow by Bigler.

20. In the Huntington version is added "among them was my brother-in-law and wife Emeline, who is my sister and is with him as laundress in the army." John W. Hess, "a fine Dutchman," later became prominent in the Utah colony. The extract from his journal is in Volume IV of the *Utah Historical Quarterly.*

The journal covering the months of November and December represents a summarization of the diary. The entries in the Huntington version seem to indicate that they were actually copied from the pocket diaries. Unfortunately several pages are missing, others are uninitialed; clippings that had been pasted into the original manuscript were simply cut out. A comparison of the two versions shows that Bigler did not omit anything essential when he prepared the copy for Bancroft.

began to grow thin and weak. To lighten up the teams the Colonel ordered packsaddles made and packed some of the strongest oxen. It was really laughable to see how they cut up with their packs on, but they soon came to it.

After leaving the Rio Grande [on the thirteenth] we marched in a Southwest course along the borders of Chihuahua towards the coppermines, but on the morning of the twenty-first of November, soon after leaving camp we were marching due south for the coppermines, where we expected to meet the foe. The Colonel was riding at the head of his command with his pilots, when he made a sudden halt and ordered his men to turn square to the right and swore he would be G–d damned if he was going all around the world to get to California. Now it had been his wish all the time to march west and cross the mountains and fall on to the head of the Gila River, but the guides had never been through that route. They had been across the country north and south of our trail and knew enough of the geography of the country that if a pass could be found, it would save a great many marches.

On the morning of the twenty-second, the Battalion was busy watering the stock until near eleven o'clock, having to take them about three miles to the place of watering. We filled our canteens and marched about eighteen miles and camped without wood or water. By sunrise the next morning we were on the march, and about 1:00 P.M. we got to water, but the spring was so weak that few of the men got water. Orders were left for the ox teams to stop here when they got up to it and camp. The main army continued without water for twelve or fifteen miles farther and camped. Oh, how men suffered that day for water, and several teams gave out. It was long after night before all the command got to camp. Here, thank God, was water plenty. We remained here the next day for the ox teams.

28

At that place we met with a lot of Spaniards who had been out trading with the Indians. Our Colonel purchased twenty mules and some of the soldiers bought some dried beef. I thought it the best meat I ever ate. On the twenty-fifth we made eighteen miles. One of our guides, Mr. Charbonneau killed a grizzly bear. His mule got away, and he shot him to get the saddle.

We continued our march and about the twenty-seventh the Colonel sent for an Indian to learn the best route across the Sierra Madre. On the evening of the twenty-eighth one of the guides brought in a chief belonging to the Apache nation, through whom the Colonel learned that there was a pass through which pack animals might go, but it was very bad. Orders were given to unload the wagons and pack. Accordingly the next day one hundred fifty pack mules were sent over the mountain with some details to pioneer and work the road. Lieutenant Dykes of Company D was sent with a company of men to guard the baggage from Indians. The distance across was some eight or ten miles and believed to be in the province of Sonora. We were two days transporting our baggage across. Empty wagons had to be let down over ledges by means of ropes, let down by hand. I think no other man but Cooke would ever have attempted to cross such a place, but he seemed to have the spirit and energy of a Bonypart.[21]

On the second of December we arrived at an old deserted Spanish village, where the inhabitants had either been killed or driven away by Indians.[22] Here the Colonel halted and sent out four hunters to kill wild cattle that once belonged to the Spaniards but had now become wild. Twelve were killed the first day, and as there was no salt in camp

---

21. At that time the common spelling and pronunciation for Napoleon Bonaparte.
22. San Bernardino Ranch on the Huaqui River.

to save it, orders were given to dry or jerk it. This was timely, for the Battalion had been short of provision ever since leaving Santa Fe, so that many began to give out by the way and had to be forced into camp by the rear guard. The sheep and cattle that had been driven along as beef and mutton for the army had become so poor that when eight ounces of it was dealt out to the soldiers, it was not half as nutritious as four ounces of good meat would be, and this too without salt to season it. It had become a common thing to eat head, heels, hide, and tripe. Even the very wool was pulled off from sheep skins that had been used under the pack saddles, and the thin hide roasted and eaten. Poor give-out beef cattle that could not be driven another inch were killed, dressed, and eaten to save men from starvation. Corporal [Sergeant Ephraim] Green of Company B had become so reduced and weak through such living, that he lost his reason.

There was one man by the name of Allen; he had slipped out from the ranks to go ahunting for antelope or deer, and got lost. He was absent for several days; had beaten back some sixty miles before he found himself. The Indians robbed him of his gun and clothes. He overtook us at this encampment naked, and almost starved to death. He had found Captain Hunter's dead horse and feasted on him so as to barely keep soul and body together.[23]

The Apaches came into our camp and traded baked roots with the soldiers. I disremember the name, but we were very fond of it. They bake it under ground by means of hot stones. It is very sweet and nutritious. Our Colonel bought a mule from them. After being in camp one day and a half, the Colonel gave orders to be on the march.

---

23. Cooke reports the return of the suspected deserter under December 3. John Allen of Company E was the only non-Mormon in the Battalion, according to Bieber (p. 131).

This quick movement prevented the soldiers from drying the large quantities of beef they had on hand [to keep it] from spoiling. He also gave orders for the guard to shoulder their knapsacks and blankets. He was told that some of the companies had their own private wagons to carry their blankets and knapsacks. His reply was he did not care a damn. They should carry them.

On the fifth we marched about twelve miles. That day there were supposed to have been seen about 4,000 wild cattle. Four were killed for beef, I believe all bulls. Captain Hunter told his wife they were young cows or heifers, to keep her from spleening against them.

On the sixth we made about fifteen miles and encamped at a place we called Little Ash Creek, a beautiful little stream of water running through an ash grove. Here we remained one day giving the guides time to hunt a camping place. When they came in, they reported there was no water short of thirty miles. At this encampment a soldier by the name of Elisha Smith died. We buried him on the banks of this creek. We made a brush heap over his grave and burned it to hide him from the savages and hungry wolves.

On the eighth we camped without water; on the ninth we made the Rio San Pedro. It affords plenty good running water and runs north, emptying I suppose into the Gila, and seems to abound with plenty of fish. Our course now was down this river and quite a lot of salmon trout was taken. Bands of wild horses were seen, as also an antelope and wild cattle.

On the tenth we camped near an old Spanish village; nothing but the old adobe walls standing, without a single inhabitant to occupy them. On the eleventh of December while marching down the San Pedro, a number of wild cattle, I believe mostly bulls, came running from the west and ran through our ranks plunging their horns into two team mules, goring them to death almost instantly and running over men. Amos Cox of Company D was thrown several feet into the air, the bull passing on, taking no farther notice of him. Cox was severely wounded in the thigh. One of those mad brutes made a charge at a soldier. The soldier to escape fell flat to the earth. The bull ran lengthwise over him, hooking down at the same time, and caught the soldiers cap on his horn, and carried it off, I suppose, in triumph. There was no timber or trees to climb out of their way, except a few scattering ones. They were soon mounted by those who were most handy. Nearly every gun was empty, for orders had been given not to carry a loaded gun in ranks. There was one man by the name of Lafayette Frost, whose gun was loaded. When one of these enraged animals made a charge at him, the Colonel seeing it hollered, "Run, run, God damn you, run." Frost, raising his gun, fired. Down dropped the bull, dead in his tracks. The Colonel turned around and swore that man was a soldier.

Some of those rascals actually made a lunge and seemingly tried to upset some of the wagons. I saw a bull make a charge, and it appeared to me that he threw the near-mule slick and clean over his off-mate. Then he plunged his horns, letting the guts out of the off-mule, while the near one received no injury. There was so much dust made that everything was out of sight for a few seconds. Ten bulls were killed that day, and several of our men wounded, but not fatal. This is known as the Great Bullfight.[24]

On the twelfth we continued our march down the river, passing several old Spanish buildings.

---

24. This was apparently the only fight in which the Battalion was engaged during the war. The "great bull fight" is discussed in detail by Cooke.

On the thirteenth at noon, the Colonel called a halt to wait for his guides, who were out hunting for the best route to a Spanish garrison some fifty or sixty miles ahead. Soon after we had camped, two of them came in and reported that the Spaniards had taken one of our men, and that they had been watching us for several days, and at the garrison there were two hundred regulars and two cannon. At 3:00 P.M. the Colonel called his Battalion out on parade and drilled his men the balance of the afternoon.

On the fourteenth we left the Rio San Pedro and marched nearly a due west course. The country seemed to be bare of timber and the land yellow. Off to our left we could see mountains covered with snow.

On the fifteenth we passed a small distillery. A few Spaniards were here making liquor from the roots of the "muscal" (as they called it).[25] The outfit seemed to be a portable affair, using raw hides for vats or tubs. After passing this place about one and a half miles, the Colonel took two Spaniards prisoners and confined them under guard. Orders also were given to fill up our canteens, as we would camp that night without water.

The next morning the man that had been taken prisoner returned,[26] and the two Spaniards set at liberty. By sunrise we were on the march for the garrison (Tucson), which was about fifteen miles distant, where we expected in all probability to have an engagement. We arrived in Tucson about the middle of the afternoon, found it was nothing but a small outpost against the Indians. The inhabitants mostly had fled on our approach, taken all the public property with them. Only a few old people and the

25. This refers to the intoxicating drink the Mexicans make from *mezcal,* a common agave-like plant of the desert. However, the drink is not made from the root, and in the Huntington version Bigler states cautiously: "I *think* it is made from the root."

26. Dr. [Stephen] Foster, assistant surgeon, interpreter, and scout.

infirm were left, and they were scared almost to death. The place looked delightful to see: the green wheat, the fruit trees, swine running about, and fowls. It was music to hear the crowing of the cocks. I suppose the reason was, we had been so long without seeing such things. There were two mills for grinding grain by mule or jackass power. The top stone revolving just as fast as the mule was of a mind to travel.

We laid here the sixteenth, and on the seventeenth we were on the march, taking a north course. After making about eight miles the Colonel halted and ordered everything to be watered, and the soldiers to fill up their canteens, as the guides said there was no more water for forty miles. We continued our march till ten o'clock at night, making some twenty five miles, and camped. When we arose in the morning, we could see a high peak in the distance ahead of us about twelve or fifteen miles. It looked like a great horn. The guides called it the Great Horn. Near there they said we could get water. Well it was a fact, we did get water, but it was not a tithing for the men. Besides the animals, every canteen was dry, and the day as hot as in the month of June at home. Orders were not to use a cup—every man take by "the word of mouth." This reminded me of the Children of Israel on one occasion lapping up the water like dogs. We then continued our march till half past ten in the night, when we came up to a small hole or two of standing water. The guides were still on ahead, with instructions that if they found water to fire a gun and make a fire as a signal. Just as we began to make camp and to unharness the teams at these holes, we heard a gun and saw the light of the fire. Orders were then given to continue, and when we got up there we were worse off than we were before, and were obliged to camp without water. Both men and teams gave out and were left behind. Myself and several others gathered our canteens and went back some two or three miles, although it was in the night and no moon. Yet we were fortunate enough to find a little water, and when we returned to camp daylight began to make its appearance in the east. The hole we found afforded about six or eight gallons of water.

The next morning being the twentieth, we found some of the mules were dead, and it was most impossible to get the teams along, and no wonder, for they had neither grass or water for two days. The country seemed to be as dry as an oven, not a piece of grass to be seen anywhere. That morning we had marched but a short distance, when we were met by one of the guides with the welcome news that about two miles and a half ahead were seven holes or ponds of water, sufficient for the whole army. As we made up to those ponds, another guide came up and reported that about one and a half miles farther on our course, he had found plenty of water and grass. We rolled up to this last spot and encamped, making that day about eight or nine miles.

The next morning, the twenty-first, before the Battalion took up the line of march, I was detailed to be the Colonel's orderly. When I went to his marquee, he was feeding his riding mule some wheat he had brought from Tucson. There was another mule that wished to share with the Colonel's, whether or no. Cooke had driven it away two or three times, but no sooner the Colonel turned his back on the mule, and back the mule would come to eat wheat. This irritated the Colonel and he bawled out to me, "Orderly, is your gun loaded?" "No, sir." "Load your gun, and I'll shoot the G—— damned mule." The thought occurred to me in a moment that he was only a little vexed and in reality did not wish to kill the mule. So I pulled out a cartridge and tore off the ball, put it in my pocket, turned down the powder, and rammed the empty cartridge down my gun. In a few minutes he came out of his tent. "Is your gun loaded?" "Yes, Sir." He took it and ran up within ten feet of the mule and let fire at its broad side. He saw the trick in a moment. He dropped the gun instantly on the ground and said "G—— damn you, you did not load that gun right," and walked straight into his marquee. I thought his bugler, Mr. Quigly, who saw the affair, would die laughing.

About eight o'clock we took up our line of march, and in the afternoon encamped on the banks of the Gila River, where the Pimas came out by the hundreds to see us. They said the Spaniards had been there and wanted them to unite with them and give us battle, and promised the Indians, if they would, they should have all the spoil. But the Pima Chief said he told them his men should not fight, that they never had shed the blood of any white man, and for this reason he was not affrighted at the coming army and had no objections to us passing through their towns.

Our Colonel bought one hundred bushels of corn for his teams. At this place we intersected General Kearny's trail, where he had come down the Gila with packs. On the twenty-second the Colonel marched eight miles and encamped in the Pima village. I understood that the Pimas were about five thousand strong and their settlements extended down the river for twenty-five miles. The Chief turned over to the Colonel some mules and store goods that had been left in his charge by General Kearny for Cooke. The Chief said that some of the Mexicans had been to him representing themselves as being part of Cooke's command and wanted the goods, saying that the Colonel had sent for them etc., but he said he did not believe it. He was glad we had come, for he believed we were the right men.

These were fine-looking Indians. They said they did not fight and steal to get their living. They seemed to have plenty of corn, beans, pumpkins, some poultry. I saw a few cattle and a good many fine ponies, some mules, and jackasses. Our Colonel bought a beef from them.

They brought into camp large quantities of corn and corn meal, wheat, and flour, also beans and squashes to trade for old shirts, old shoes, pants, vests, beads and buttons. They would not have money. They said it was of no use to them. I saw their women grinding wheat by hand, the largest stone about fifteen inches by twenty, a little scooped. The grain was put into this and rubbed with another stone, about the same length and six inches wide. They raised cotton and manufactured it into blankets and breech-clouts. On the twenty-fifth the boys bought melons to have it to say they have watermelons to eat on Christmas day. That morning orders were given for the Battalion not to eat any corn, either public or private. What that was for, I do not know, unless the Colonel was afraid his men would make themselves sick by eating, for many had bought of the Indians corn to boil. It was of a quality that was easily cooked and when cooked had the flavor of young corn. They had gotten beans from the Pimas to boil with their corn. This was also forbidden, and orders were to leave the whole of it.

That day we left the river and traveled a southwest course around some mountains and over a heavy sandy road, falling on to the Gila again in about forty miles, thus cutting off about one hundred miles. We marched till eight o'clock at night, and camped without water, and I may say, without grass.

The twenty-sixth we made the Gila. The road was very sandy.

III.

ACROSS CALIFORNIA
TO SAN DIEGO: 1846-1847

December 27. Made about eight miles. The road was sandy and bad, and it was a marvel how the teams stood it as well as they did with scarcely any grass for them. In fact, the country along here seemed to have no grass except in small patches and far between, not sufficient for ten mules, besides two hundred or three hundred, and about two hundred sheep and forty head of beef cattle. These cattle and sheep were brought from the Santa Fe country and were now as poor, as the saying is, as Job's turkey. Indeed, they were nothing but skin and bones. In the forepart of our journey I had an idea that our ox teams would stand a long journey better than mules, but the oxen have long since given out and been killed for beef and eaten up. Oxen must have grass or grain, but a mule will live on the bark of trees.

December 28. This day the Colonel dispatched two guides and a few men to General Kearny, as I understood, for fresh mules, and [they were] to hasten back as quick as possible, as the Colonel's teams were giving out daily for want of flesh.

December 29. Marched over some bad road, sandy and rocky, and over hills. We passed a mass of rocks on our right, carved all over with birds, beasts, serpents, and men. I suppose done by Indians.[1]

December 31. Made about twelve miles and encamped

1. These are the same hieroglyphs which Emory observed on November 16 and describes in his *Notes*. Noticed also by Bliss.

on the river. Here was a very little grass and a pond of salt water.

January 1, 1847. This morning in gathering up the mules we found four dead. About seven o'clock we were on the march. We met some Mexicans moving on pack mules from San Diego to Chihuahua. They met General Kearny eighteen days ago near the "Pueblo." [2] That day we made about fifteen miles, and at that encampment the Colonel ordered that two wagons be unloaded, the beds put into the river to see if they would leak, as he said they were made to be water tight. They were found to be water tight, and on the second the beds were lashed side by side, and the two wagons and their baggage put on board and a few men to man the boat, and sent down the Gila with orders to haul in every night and camp with the command.

On the third, we made about fifteen miles. The boat did not get up with us.[3]

January 4. This morning the Colonel sent up the river to learn what the matter was, and learned that the boat had run aground, and it was doubtful about getting along. We marched down the river about eight miles and camped, and as there was so little grass, orders were for us to fell small cottonwood trees for the mules to feed upon the bark. Two were found dead this morning. It was said by some for want of water, as the Colonel had given orders to the teamsters some time ago not to water the animals without orders, or at the sound of the bugle.

January 5. Made a short march and encamped on a small patch of grass. One of the guides said the weather was

2. Pueblo stands here for Pueblo de los Angeles. From now on the modern name Los Angeles will be used to avoid confusion with Pueblo, Colorado.

3. The boat under Lieutenant Stoneman had been grounded and only part of the valuable provisions was subsequently saved.

so hot when he passed here last September with an express to Santa Fe that he had to travel in the night. I have not seen ice this winter thicker than a knife blade. This morning the Colonel sent a corporal and a few privates with mules up the river, as it was reported that the provision was put ashore and left on the bank of the river, except some corn and bacon that was left on a sand bar in the middle of the river. Late at night the boat arrived with very little on board.

January 7. Made about ten miles and encamped at the end of a mountain called by the guides the Devils Point.[4] The Colonel sent out some men to work a road around this point. This chain appeared to be nothing but a mass of rocks, not a single spear of any thing could be seen growing on it, and peaks towering perpendicular up for aught I know for more than two thousand feet high. The Colonel sent all the animals across the river to get a little grass, as there was none on the south side. The river is about two hundred yards wide.

January 8. We encamped near the mouth of the river. The boat did not get up last night and the Corporal with his men that was sent back for the provision has not returned.

January 9. This morning two wagons and harness was left. The teams are very weak. One was found dead this morning. Although the Colonel bought corn of the Indians and feeds them one quart once a day, it is not enough. Orders were given last evening for the Quartermaster to weigh the provisions, and he reported only nine days of half rations, and it was estimated to be at least twelve days march to the nearest settlement in California. We marched today about twelve miles and encamped on the bank of the Colorado River. At this camp the Colonel gave orders

4. Gila Mountains.

to gather and sack up a large quantity of "Muskeet." [5]
The tree is a shrubbery and bears a fruit hanging in clusters, and to me resembles so many caterpillars or a lot of screws hanging together. Some of the Battalion gathered and ground a lot of it in their coffee mills and mixed it half and half with flour and made bread of it. It was sweet and ate very well. The mules were fond of this fruit and so were many of the soldiers, but it bound them up so tight that some became frightened and thought they never would be delivered and would have to send for the doctor. Late at night the boat got up.

January 10. Today the Corporal and part of his men caught up with the camp with part of the flour; the bacon they did not find. The other men were still back in search of the meat and some flour left still farther up the river that was not found. This day was mostly spent in crossing the Colorado River. The river is about half a mile wide at this point, not very deep, but runs swift and rather muddy like the Missouri. Two mules got drowned in crossing.

January 11. The boat ran all last night ferrying our baggage over, and today about noon everything was gotten across except some wagons and harness that were left. In the afternoon made about fifteen miles. The road was sandy and some of the teams gave out. Two wagons were left and the baggage put on mules and packed. It was late

5. In the Huntington version many of the details are recorded under the eighth which are here given under the ninth. On the other hand a detailed description of the bad effect of eating the ground-up mesquite beans is given and dated the tenth in the Huntington version. Some of the soldiers were so frightened that they believed they could not be delivered *without sending for doctor Sanderson!* The mesquite is the common name for several species of the genus *Prosopis,* an acacia, valued by Indians and desert dwellers for their seed pods. While in the Bancroft and Huntington versions the story is told in great detail, the Utah and Hittell versions make no mention of it. Standage records that "mules and men are very fond of this," but does not speak of its effect.

when we made camp. Here General Kearny had dug a well, but it was dry, and a dead wolf was in it. A few details were made and the well sunk a few feet deeper when water was got. Another well was also dug by our men. In going about ten feet, plenty of water was had.

The next morning two more wagons were left. Here Major Cloud,[6] our paymaster, cached a trunk of tools and some other articles. The probability was that all the wagons left on the California side would be sent for from San Diego. We marched that day about ten miles.

On the thirteenth we made about fifteen miles. Here was another well dug by General Kearny, but like the other was dry and had four dead wolves in it. It was soon cleaned out and dug deeper. Also another well at the same time was being dug, and plenty of water was had for the whole command. The men that were left on the other side of the Colorado hunting for the pork and flour had not come up, and there was fear that they were taken or killed by Indians.[7]

On the morning of the fourteenth, twenty-four men were detailed with picks and shovels to go ahead twenty-four miles with one of the guides to dig for water. That night we encamped without water.

By sunrise the next morning we were on the march and by ten or eleven o'clock we were up with the details.[8] They

6. Not listed in the rosters by Tyler or Golder. Major Jeremiah H. Cloud of Missouri was "additional paymaster." On August 4, 1847, while riding with Sutter near Sutter's Fort, he was thrown from his horse and killed (*New Helvetia Diary;* Gudde, *Sutter,* p. 181).

7. From here on the Bancroft and Huntington copies can be collated with the Hittell version. The latter was reduced by Bigler (or Hittell) to a minimum. The entries between January 10 and 21 are missing in the Huntington version.

8. In charge of Lieutenant George Stoneman (Hittell and Utah). Stoneman, often mentioned in Cooke's Journal, was later general of cavalry in the Civil War, and was governor of California, 1883-1887.

42

had dug deep but unfortunately scarcely any water was had or found! Here we met with the two guides and the men that were sent to General Kearny from Gila with a number of fresh mules and horses and a few beef cattle. A few Spaniards and Indians came with the drove. Most of the animals had never been broke and were tolerably wild, and it was diverting to the soldiers to see how handy the Spaniards were in throwing the lassoe and catching the animals the Colonel wanted to use. They made forth with some of them to work in the teams. One of the fresh beeves was killed and dressed, with orders to cook and eat and be on the march in one hour and a half for the next water and grass. The Battalion was now entirely out of flour and salt. The coffee and sugar had been gone some time. So small was the stream of water at this place none could be had to cook with, or even to fill our canteens. We hastily broiled our meat and were soon on the march for water, and it was said to be only about twenty miles. When night came on, we camped without water and without supper. Orders were given to tie up the teams and to guard the pack animals in a close quarter, and be on the march again by midnight.

Accordingly we were on the move and by three o'clock P.M. we reached water [after] some forty or forty-five miles instead of twenty. The road was very sandy. Twenty mules gave out and were left to take care of themselves. A great many men suffered that day for want of water— tired, weak, faint and hungry—not eating anything since the day before about noon. One mule got away with a pack on. I believe it never was found.

The seventeenth we continued our march for about sixteen miles. An ox gave out and was left, but a few who had fallen back killed him, struck fire, roasted [him], and ate without bread or salt, until forced away by the rear guard. It was late at night before all the command got up to camp.

January 18. The Colonel laid by, and the men were busy washing and mending clothes, cleaning guns [which were] filled with sand and dust. Late in the evening an Indian came with a letter from General Kearny to Cooke. There were camp rumors that Kearny had a battle or two with the Spaniards and was slightly wounded, and the General and Commodore Stockton had united their forces and were on the march for Los Angeles, one of the strong-holds of the enemy. But know what the contents of the letter were, I did not.[9]

On the nineteenth we crossed over a mountain. Ropes were fastened to the wagons, and every man that could get ahold pulled and pushed until all got over, falling into a small valley, where for the first time on our tramp, I noticed the wild sage. We soon left this by turning to our right up a little creek but dry, at the head of which we wished to cross the mountain. But the mountain soon closed upon us on each side, that our pass became more narrow than our wagons, and we were obliged to take some of the wagons apart. But while we were unloading and making preparations, a lot of men went to work and cut through the rocks so as to admit the passage of our wagons without taking them to pieces. We encamped that night on the top of the mountain without wood and water.

The next morning by daylight the camp was on the move and after marching about five miles, came to a nice running little stream of water. Here we halted and break-

9. Bigler and the Mormons would have rejoiced if they had known the content of the letter. After the so-called "Battle of the Mesa" on the ninth the Californians were dispersed, and the remnants surrendered four days later to Frémont at Cahuenga. Thus the Battalion could enter California as conqueror without having fired a single shot at the enemy.

fasted and watered the animals, after which we went some seven or eight miles and encamped in a beautiful valley; plenty of water, and young grass growing finely. Everything around began to look like there was life in it. The mountains began to show timber (pine) and along the creeks the live oak was abundant. This evening one of the men, that was back on the Gila after the provision, got in. He had left his company this morning with some of the flour back where we had camped night before last. He reported they did not find all the flour; believed the Indians must have gotten it. Their mules had given out, preventing them from overtaking the camp, and at this time were unable to travel any further. At midnight some men and mules were sent back to bring them up.

January 21. Marched ten miles, when we arrived at Mr. Warner's, the first settlement, and encamped.[10] The Colonel got some fresh beef cattle of this gentleman and issued four and one half pounds of beef to the soldier per day. This did very well, although rather flat eating without salt or bread. The Colonel laid over at this place all the next day. I understood that Mr. Warner owned a ranch some fifteen leagues square with three thousand head of cattle on it. While lying here, some of our boys found a hot spring about half a mile from camp, but after the water had run a few rods from the head, it became cool enough to bathe in, and the most of the Battalion had a good time washing off.[11]

January 23. Orders were given to be on the march; [it]

---

10. In those years Warner's Ranch played about the same role for the southern trail as Sutter's Fort played for the northern route.

11. The Huntington version has a long entry under the date of the twenty-second about the march to Los Angeles and San Diego. The soldiers hoped to be shipped from San Diego to San Francisco and "the boys feel that they would like a ride of that sort after having footed it so far."

was said for Los Angeles. Today the company that had gone up the Gila after the provision, all got up to camp with their flour and one sack of bacon. The flour was soon weighed out. There was only one pound and a quarter to the soldier. There were twelve hundred pounds of flour put aboard the boat. I would not wonder at all if the truth was told that they "played off" on the Colonel as well as on the whole command, and were in no hurry about overtaking the army, for if they did, they would soon come on short 'lowance, and while they had plenty they were in no haste.

It commenced to rain in the night and rained hard, too, and on the morning of the twenty-fourth several mules were found dead. The Colonel marched about two and one half miles where was plenty of timber to shelter the mules from the wind. It was still raining and it stormed most all night. The wind blew a hurricane. Hardly a tent was found the next morning standing. Sam Hill, how it did rain! It was cold, and it seemed that it would kill every animal in camp. A good many hats were lost.[12]

The twenty-fifth it was clear and nice—made that day some twelve miles and camped in one of the prettiest valleys I thought I ever had seen. As we marched along today we could see on our right about fifty miles a mountain covered with snow that fell during the previous night. This evening an express came from General Kearny for us to go to San Diego. This order seemed to please the soldiers, as they understood from the express man that a ship was expected every day to arrive at that place from the Sandwich

---

12. In the Huntington version Bigler records for the first time that the Pueblo "is sometimes called Los Angeles, the meaning of which I believe is the City of Angels." This belief is still prevalent although the name is an abbreviation of the Old Spanish name, *Nuestra Señora Reina de los Angeles de Porciuncula.*

Islands laden with provisions. She had been out forty-two days and was only to be gone forty.[13]

January 26. This morning we took up our line of march for San Diego and in fording a creek that was flush from the late rain and ran swift as a mill tail and pretty rough, every officer except the Colonel got a complete ducking. Their mules fell from under them. The guides did not escape and every soldier had to wade. It was rather a wet time. The Colonel soon went into camp, where wood was plenty and a kind of general drying off took place. We saw some fine herds of fat cattle. The Colonel ordered some of them to be taken for beef. Doctor Sanderson advised the camp not to boil their beef but to broil it; not having any salt, it would be better for us. [This] was carried out I believe to the very letter.

January 27. While on the march today, we were overtaken with an express from General Kearny for us to march to a certain mission for quarters. We also learned from the expressman (I think his name was Walker) that we had taken a wrong road and had traveled some ten or twelve miles out of our way. Our course was now southwest. The whole country appeared to be alive with large bands of horses, mules, and jackasses, and the valleys and hills covered with herds of cattle, and along the larger streams any amount of geese, crane, and brants. We passed San Luis Rey and turned a little to our left over a hill, from the top of which for the first time we got sight of the Pacific Ocean about four or five miles in the distance, and at night camped near the seashore.

January 28. Marched about fifteen miles over broken

---

13. In the Huntington version Bigler records that in this pretty valley the Battalion came close to a fight. He had felt unwell and lagged behind, but the others told him that they encountered a large body of Indians ready to attack. However, they had withdrawn when they discovered that the soldiers were Americans, not Mexicans.

country but alive with stock. I heard one of the guides say he knew one man who owned twelve thousand head of cattle. In many places there were scores and perhaps hundreds of acres of wild oats growing, looking as green as a wheat field at home in the month of May. I noticed another thing. Since coming near the ocean we have some dew, which was not the case in New Mexico, and, indeed, if I remember right, we had none soon after leaving Fort Leavenworth. Carcasses do not seem to rot in these countries as soon as they do in the United States, but literally dry up like a mummy, and I do not know but the people live longer for I have seen some Mexicans and Indians who looked to me as if they were as old as the everlasting hills. We made about twenty miles when we arrived at the San Diego Mission, where we expected to go into quarters.[14]

January 30. The soldiers busy cleaning out the mission rooms. They were very dirty and full of fleas as they have not been occupied except by Indians for some time. Here are three nice vineyards and a number of olive trees. I judge from the appearance that the missionaries have had plenty of wine and oil.

January 31. Several of the boys or soldiers went down to San Diego about four or five miles distant. On their return they said there were in the harbor two men-of-war, one merchant vessel, a whaler, and a schooner, and that General Kearny had sailed the day before for the Bay of San Francisco. I also understood that Captain Hunt had written a letter to General Kearny stating to him the condition of the Mormon Battalion: that we were destitute of clothing and barefooted and without provisions except some beef, and that without salt. There were no provisions at San Diego. The ship from the Sandwich Islands had

---

14. The other versions have entries for January 29, when the Battalion actually entered San Diego.

not arrived. They were daily expecting the arrival of three vessels from New York laden with supplies. They had left that port last August.[15]

IV.

THE VANISHING DAYS
OF MEXICAN RULE: 1847

Orders were now given, for some cause, for us to be marched back to San Luis Rey or San Luis Mission, and there go into quarters.[1]

February 1. We took up our line of march and arrived on the third about noon at that place, some forty miles. This is a handsome situation and good buildings sufficient to accommodate a thousand soldiers, first-rate barracks. Here also were two vineyards, a number of olive trees, pepper trees, and peach trees. The latter were in bloom. The Battalion was some three days cleaning out and cleaning up the barracks. Here too were plenty of fleas. After we had been in quarters about a week, we were then called out every day on duty to drill a few hours.[2]

---

15. The entries in the Huntington version of these days are more detailed but add nothing important.

1. The Mission San Luis Rey, founded 1797, is about forty miles north of San Diego on the road to Los Angeles.

2. The Huntington version has daily entries between the first to the seventh. The only additional interesting item is that no priest was around the mission, and the Indians "worship the Great Spirit in their own way." The entries from February 7 to May 12 (pp. 88 to 99) are missing from the Huntington version. The Standage journal has daily entries and records faithfully every daily drill, which is mentioned by Bigler in this entry only.

On the tenth the Colonel sent Lieutenant [George W.] Omen and ten men [of Company A] and fourteen mules up towards Los Angeles to meet some Spaniards and help them in with a load of flour for the Battalion.[3]

On the nineteenth the Lieutenant returned with 2100 lbs. of unbolted flour, and reported that we could be furnished in a few days with 5000 more.

On the twentieth the Colonel got word that a vessel laden with provisions had landed at San Diego from the Sandwich Islands. The Colonel sent a few teams and wagons forthwith for "grub."

On the twenty sixth the wagons returned laden with pork, flour, sugar, and coffee.

March 8. This evening an express arrived from San Diego. The particulars I did not learn, but there was talk in camp that a French vessel had arrived at San Diego and that Colonel Cooke got a paper stating that General Santa Anna had borrowed twenty-five million dollars of the Roman Catholics [4] and had entrenched himself awaiting the arrival of General Taylor.

On the fourteenth of March, our Colonel received orders from General Kearny to send one company to San Diego, as he had given orders for the Regulars to leave that post and go to Los Angeles. The next morning Company B took up their line of march for that place, where they arrived about noon on the seventeenth.

---

3. In the Hittell and Utah versions this information is given under the date of February 14; likewise in Standage. Hence Bigler doubtless erred in this instance. In addition, the Hittell and Utah versions have this information under February 14, a Sunday: "We had preaching today by George P. Dykes, who took his text from the second chapter of Daniel. He was followed by Captain Jefferson Hunt, who exhorted us to be obedient to our officers and to God, and told us that our Colonel permitted us to hold services every Sunday and to invite strangers."

4. Apparently one of the customary war rumors. Neither in Hittell or Utah versions, nor in Standage or Bliss.

PHOTOGRAPH BY COURTESY OF BANCROFT LIBRARY

SANTA FE IN 1846 FROM W. H. EMORY, *Notes of a Military Reconnoissance* (1848)

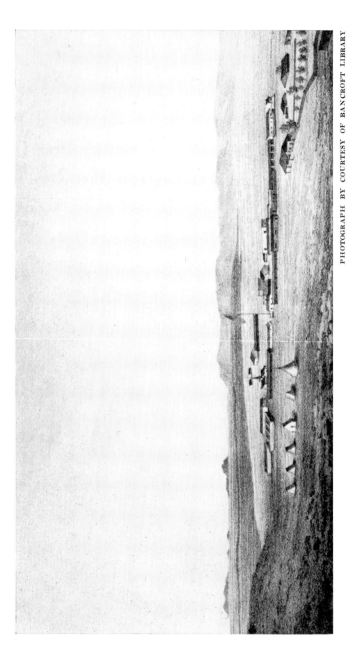

SAN DIEGO IN 1846 FROM W. H. EMORY, *Notes of a Military Reconnoissance* (1848)

On the day following, our Captain received a letter from the Colonel giving information that he was on the march with Company C, D, and E to Los Angeles to take possession of that place, and Company A was left to keep San Luis Rey. This morning the marines all went aboard and we took possession of the fort, which was situated on a bluff about one fourth of a mile from the village, with seven pieces of artillery to defend it. The *Congress*, commanded by Commodore Stockton, was lying in San Diego harbor. On our arrival on the Pacific Coast the Colonel issued the following—Order No. 1, Headquarters, Mormon Battalion, Mission of San Diego, January 30th, 1847: [5]

The Lieutenant colonel commanding congratulates the Battalion on their safe arrival on the shores of the Pacific ocean and the conclusion of its march of over two thousand miles. History may be searched in vain for an equal march of infantry. Nine-tenths of it has been through a wilderness where nothing but savages and wild beasts are found, or deserts where, from want of water, there is no living creature. There, with almost hopeless labor we have dug deep wells, which the future traveler will enjoy. Without a guide who had traversed them, we have ventured into trackless prairies where water was not found for several marches. With crowbar, pick, and ax in hand, we have worked our way over mountains which seemed to defy aught save the wild goat, and have hewed a passage through a chasm of living rock more narrow than our wagons. To bring these first wagons to the Pacific, we have preserved the strength of our mules by herding them over large tracts, which you have laboriously guarded without loss. The garrison of four presidios of Sonora concentrated within the walls of Tucson, gave us no pause. We drove them out with their artillery, but our intercourse with the citizens was unmarked by a single act of injustice. Thus marching half-naked

5. This order has been corrected here according to the official text at the end of Cooke's *Journal*. Somewhat exaggerated in its praise, it has naturally found its way into the Mormon literature. In the Hittell and Utah versions it is printed under the date of February 18.

and half-fed, and living upon wild animals, we have discovered and made a road of great value to our country.

Arrived at the first settlement of California after a single day's rest, you cheerfully turned off from the route to this point of promised repose, to enter upon a campaign and meet, as we believed, the approach of the enemy, and this, too, without salt to season your sole subsistence of fresh meat.

Lieutenant A. J. Smith and George Stoneman, of the 1st dragoons, have shared and given valuable aid in all these labors.

Thus, volunteers, you have exhibited some high and essential qualifications of veterans. But much remains undone. Soon you will turn your strict attention to the drill, to system and order, to forms, also, which are all necessary to the soldier.

> By order of Lieut. Col. P.S. Geo. Cooke
> P. C. Merrill, *Adjutant.*

On the thirty first of March two wagons came to San Diego for groceries for the troops at Los Angeles. We learn from them that the mountain Indians had sallied into the settlements and committed depredations, had killed some fifteen or twenty Spaniards—men, women, and children—and that the dragoons from Los Angeles had gone out to fight them.[6]

On the second of April rumors were in camp that our Captain had received a letter from the Colonel stating that General Taylor had fought one of the greatest battles ever fought in America. He had scaled the walls of the enemy with four thousand against ten thousand and gained the victory. The Mexicans lost 1400 and Taylor five hundred, and Santa Anna was still making preparations to fight.[7]

On the eighth the ship *Barnstable* arrived from San Francisco, bringing forty barrels of flour for Company

---

6. The Hittell and Utah versions have several entries between the fifteenth and thirtieth about the life and duties in San Diego.

7. This refers to the arrival of the news of Taylor's victory at Buena Vista on February 23.

B, our Captain receiving a letter at the same time from the Colonel to give his men full rations of flour and one pound and half beef per day to the soldiers, and tells the Captain that Oregon and California are united and form the tenth division in the military department.[8]

On the sixteenth, a mail from the "Bay of San Francisco" arrived, and I understood that a regular mail route was now established from here (San Diego) to that point, and the round trip could be made in fourteen days, and this mail was the first trip made.[9]

On the twenty-seventh we had the painful duty of paying our last respects to Captain [Jesse D.] Hunter's wife, who died on the previous evening. She had lately been confined in child birth and has left an infant babe. Her funeral was preached by Elder William Hyde.[10]

On the second of May word reached San Diego that Colonel Cooke and Frémont were at loggerheads and that Cooke's men were busy making cartridges, expecting an attack from Frémont, who was at the head of some three or four hundred men. The whole truth of this affair I never fully learned but the understanding at the time was that General Kearny had ordered Cooke, with part of his command, to go to Los Angeles and take possession of that post with all the artillery. Frémont at first refused, as he was there in possession, and made some threats what he

---

8. "Sunday, April 4. Elder William Hyde, our sergeant, preached today. Many of the citizens, and officers, and sailors of the vessels in the harbor were present" (Hittell). Similar in the Utah version.

9. On the fourteenth a sailor from the U. S. Frigate *Congress* was baptized, "probably the first baptism in California of a Mormon convert." (In Hittell and Utah versions but not in Bancroft version.)

10. The Hittell and Utah versions record under the date of the twenty-eighth that a pitiful cripple was found begging in the streets of San Diego and that he was one of Frémont's men [?] who had lived in the mountains for seven years; he admitted he was a member of the mob that had participated in the Haun's Mill massacre of the Mormons in Missouri, October 30, 1838.

was going to do with the damned Mormons, but certain it was that there was some misunderstanding and threats had been made.[11]

On the sixth, we heard that the Americans had taken Vera Cruz after eleven days fighting.

On the tenth, myself, Ephraim Green, Israel Evans, Jesse Martin, and Hyrum Mount went out from San Diego about eight miles (having the privilege from our Captain) to cut cord wood for burning brick at the rate of two dollars per cord.

On the eleventh, Albert Dunham was buried. The doctor said he had an ulcer on his brain. There was talk that an express had arrived from Washington giving the news that Captain Frémont was appointed Governor of California, that General Kearny and Colonel Cooke were ordered home,[12] and that General Doniphan, who was at Santa Fe, had a battle with the Spaniards and Indians near Abagus (or some such name) [Rio Abajo]. The Spaniards and Indians had lost about three hundred, while Doniphan only a few, and more, that while the General was on the march to Chihuahua, he was attacked by twelve hundred Spaniards and flogged them severely.[13] We also had word to the effect that a lot of Indians came

11. The somewhat undignified controversy between Kearny and Frémont, backed by Stockton, can be found in any history of California. A good account is given in Theodore H. Hittell's *History of California,* Book VII.

In Huntington and Utah versions it is recorded under May 3 that Major Cloud came with the Battalion's six-month pay; and under May 4, that the "Haun Mill beggar" was convicted of stealing a pocket knife.

12. This rumor was probably spread by the same friends of Frémont who tried their best to get him appointed, directly from Washington, D. C., as governor of California.

13. Colonel Alexander W. Doniphan, who commanded in New Mexico, stood in high esteem among the Mormons because he had protested the treatment of the Mormons at Far West, Missouri, in 1838. The two victories referred to were at El Brazito, December 25, 1846, and Sacramento, February 28.

to Los Angeles and made a treaty with Colonel Cooke and expressed a desire to live in peace with all people, but on their return to their homes in the mountains, they had robbed a ranch and the Colonel had sent Lieutenant Thompson of Company C with twenty men to pursue them. They were soon overtaken and fired upon, killing six. The Indians returned the fire, wounding three of Thompson's men.

On the sixteenth of May a mail arrived from up the country,[14] and the news was that General Kearny and Colonel Cooke were to leave the next morning for home, taking twelve men from the Mormon Battalion for life guards, and that General Stevenson and Colonel Mason take the command of the army, and that Captain Hunt of Company A was appointed major.[15]

May 30. The mail came in and some of the boys got letters, and the news was to the effect that a lot of Mormon families (who had come around in the ship *Brooklyn*) had settled in the Monterey country and had [put] in one hundred forty-five acres of wheat and several acres of corn and potatoes, and Sam Brannan had gone to meet

---

14. That is, from Monterey.

15. Colonel Jonathan D. Stevenson, who had arrived in April with his New York Volunteers. He became commandant of the southern district. His troops likewise saw no action, but like the Mormons many became well-known pioneers after the discovery of gold.

Colonel Richard B. Mason succeeded Kearny as military governor of California, on May 31, 1847.

The Hittell version records under the date of May 26 that the Mormons had begun to purchase and break wild horses and mules for their trip to Salt Lake. Bigler writes this in retrospect, for nowhere else had mention been made that the Battalion was informed that Brigham Young had decided to found the colony by Great Salt Lake. None of the earlier versions record Salt Lake as the future colony. See footnote 19.

The Huntington version has details about earning money by cutting wood and fishing in the ocean; also states that an Indian was publicly whipped in the square of San Diego for having attempted to kill his mother.

the emigration (Brigham Young and Company). Mr. Brannan with about two hundred Mormons had come round the Horn in the Ship *Brooklyn* and arrived the previous August or September in the Bay of San Francisco. They chartered that vessel at New York and set sail February 4th, 1846, and it strikes me, though I am not sure, they chartered that vessel for six thousand dollars per month, and I have understood that at the time they landed, there were only nine houses in the city, adobes, the most of them poor at that.[16]

On the fourth of June the mail brought us word that General Taylor had whipped old Santa Anna, and our company gave a cheer of twenty rounds of cannon.[17]

On the twenty-third of June Colonel Stevenson from Los Angeles came to San Diego to raise volunteers from our Company to serve six or twelve months longer. He got the promise of quite a number to re-inlist after they were discharged from their present enlistment, and Lieutenant Cliff [Robert Clift] of Company C was appointed this day to be alcalde of this place.

On the twenty-eighth, William Garner completed a well that he and I dug for Captain Fitch, an old resident of San Diego, and on the twenty-ninth, I tended a brick mason, who paved a yard and walk way with brick for a Spanish gentleman.[18]

16. See sections vi and vii on Brannan and the *Brooklyn*.
17. Doubtless refers to Scott's victory at Cerro Gordo, April 18, 1847. According to Bliss, the news did not arrive until the fourteenth. "The Catholic Church had a few less Glass than usual when we ceased firing."

Hittell, June 21: "The ship *Vandalia* sailed for Boston, with a mail on which I have sent letters to friends in the States. Today I worked at digging a well, our captain having permitted to take such jobs."

18. According to the Huntington version, they started the well on the twenty-second, and Bigler received a daily wage of one dollar. He believed that brick work was introduced into California by the Mormons.

Henry Delano Fitch was master of several trading vessels and at that time *juez de paz* in San Diego. The Spanish gentleman was Juan Bandini, a well-known political figure who sided early with the United States.

July 4. At daylight five pieces of cannon were fired off to salute the day of American Independence. After that the boys shouldered their muskets by order of Mr. James Sly, whom they had selected for their Captain for the present occasion, marched in order, and gave the officers of Company B and the citizens of San Diego a hearty salute. This seemed to please the inhabitants of the town so well that they brought out their bottles of wine and *aguardiente* and called upon the boys to help themselves to all they could drink, and the day passed off nicely. In the evening Captain Hunter and Sergeant Hyde who had gone with Colonel J. D. Stevenson up to Los Angeles to lend their influence in raising volunteers, returned. The boys shouldered their pieces and marched to their quarters and gave them a hearty cheer.[19]

With the arrival at San Diego, the march of the Mormon Battalion came to an end. It was one of the most notable feats ever achieved by an infantry unit. Mormon historians have naturally exaggerated the accomplishments of the Battalion. It was doubtless the longest march ever undertaken by an infantry unit on the North American continent, and the great role which the Battalion and its individual members have played in the history of the American West deserves recognition and appreciation. But it was not more than another chapter in the forward movement of the American Frontier, full of heroism and suffering.

19. According to the Huntington version, only thirteen out of three hundred reënlisted. More important is another entry under the same date which shows that the Battalion at that time did not yet know that Brigham Young had decided for the Great Salt Lake region: "All hands were now busy making preparations to leave for their homes wherever that was; whether on Bear River, California, or Vancouver Island up in the British possession. For the truth is we do not know where President Young and the Church is."

While the five hundred Mormons were on the march, the future history of their Church was decided. After most Saints had left Nauvoo by the end of April, 1846, and were encamped in the "Camps of Israel" in present-day Iowa, the remaining inhabitants were harassed by the people of Illinois and finally forced to leave the state. On September 17, 1846, when the Battalion was on the march from Fort Leavenworth to Santa Fe, the last Mormons crossed the Mississippi to join their brethren on the Missouri.

In the meantime the idea of settling in California had received a new impetus. On February 4, 1846, two hundred and thirty-eight Saints from the Atlantic seaboard had embarked on the rather dilapidated ship *Brooklyn* in New York. Samuel Brannan, the enterprising Mormon who knew how to amalgamate religion and business, was the soul of this bold enterprise. After a stormy voyage around Cape Horn the ship load of pioneers were saved in the nick of time by stopping at Juan Fernández, the Pacific group of isles, one of which numerous thoughtless scholars of literary history still call the "Robinson Crusoe Island."

From there the ship proceeded to the Hawaiian Islands to unload the cargo for which Brannan had contracted to help finance the trip. Here the seafarers heard for the first time of the war between the United States and Mexico. The realization that California would soon be a part of the country they had left filled the hearts of many Mormons with apprehension. Not the enterprising Sam. The American squadron, anchoring off Honolulu, did not make any attempt to prevent the *Brooklyn* from proceeding to the San Francisco Bay. On the contrary it seems that Commodore Stockton, ready with his fleet for a naval attack upon California, encouraged Brannan. The latter bought rifles and, ignorant of what had transpired in the meantime, began to dream of conquering California and making it a Mormon territory within the United States. Thus, unaware of each other, two armed units of Mormons were descending upon California in the same year. On the very day Allen's battalion reached Fort Leavenworth, the members of Brannan's battalion gazed through the morning haze upon the Golden Gate.

Both voluntary units came too late—doubtless to the great relief of most of the members—to shed any blood in the Mexican War for the glory of the United States and the benefit of the Church.

When the *Brooklyn* sailed into the harbor of the little village of Yerba Buena the men were greeted by the U. S. Sloop *Portsmouth*, whose commander, John B. Montgomery, had hoisted the Stars and Stripes nine days before.

Brannan was disappointed, but his unquenchable spirit rose to the occasion. The arrival of the *Brooklyn* had added enough inhabitants to the sleepy settlement to make the Latter-day Saints the deciding element in what was soon to become San Francisco, and Brannan was optimistic enough to believe that he had established the nucleus for a Mormon California.

The first step was the establishment of an agricultural settlement. Shortly after the arrival of the *Brooklyn* Brannan had selected a site for the community farm, New Hope. In September he led the first twenty settlers to the spot on the north bank of the Stanislaus, a short distance from its junction with the San Joaquin.

Next he set up the press he had brought from New York, and on January 9, 1847, he published the first newspaper of San Francisco, the *California Star*. In his editorial policy as well as in his other activities he was careful not to stress the Mormon front of his many-sided personality—something that was not difficult for a man more interested in making money than in spreading the new gospel.

But his most important task was still ahead of him: to convince Brigham Young and the Elders of the Church that California was the place for the new Zion.

V.

FROM LOS ANGELES
TO DONNER LAKE: 1847

Our time was now drawing near when we were to leave for Los Angeles to receive our discharge. The citizens of San Diego insisted that we enlist again. They said it was their wish to have us remain and told us that they had learned that we were peaceable and quiet, and minded our own business, and were industrious and had greatly improved their little town. Some of the leading men of the place told us that when they heard that a set of Mormon soldiers were coming to San Diego, they had a great notion to pack up and leave the place, for they had been told that the Mormons would steal everything they could lay their hands on. Not only that but their women would be in danger of being insulted by them.

On the sixth [of July], the citizens (so I was informed) sent a petition to Colonel Stevenson to send a company of Mormon soldiers to be stationed there as soon as he could raise them. They seemed to be favorable to the American

60

flag and said they knew they will catch hell soon after we leave.[1]

On the eighth, our brick masons finished laying up the first brick house in that place and for all I know the first in California.[2] The building, I believe, was designed to be used for a courthouse and schoolhouse. The inhabitants came together, set out a table well spread with wines and different kinds of drinks that the place could afford and invited the masons (Messrs. Philander Colton and Rufus Stoddard) and everybody else to help themselves, and there was a jolly old time and everything passed off first rate. Some fifteen or twenty wells had been dug by our boys and walled up with brick, and Sidney Willis made a few pumps, which was also a new thing, and put in some of their wells. The brick was made by Colton, Stoddard, Henry Wilcox, and William Garner. Mr. Colton told me they put up a kiln of over forty thousand bricks.

On the ninth we took up our line of march for the Pueblo or Los Angeles, where we arrived on the fifteenth, and on the sixteenth of July, the battalion was mustered out of service.[3] But as they were beating up for volunteers, a great many of the Mormon boys volunteered to serve six months longer and were sent to San Diego under Captain [Daniel C.] Davis.

On the nineteenth, the Battalion was paid off all except our transportation money, all of which we never got (to this day), and on the twentieth, a few went up the

1. In a lengthy entry under July 5 in the Huntington version, Bigler proudly enumerates the improvements made by Mormons in San Diego.
2. The Huntington version records under July 8 that after finishing the work the boys took a bath in the bay and that Bigler bought a horse for five dollars.
3. The Huntington version has daily entries of the march to Los Angeles and a description of the town, which Bigler liked much better than did Standage (in his entry under May 2).

San Pedro River [4] about three miles and hunted out a camping place. There we began to gather, to organize and prepare for a general move for Bear River Valley (as we called it then), where we expected to meet or find our people of The Church.[5] Most of the boys had already bought animals to pack and ride and had everything ready for a move as soon as we got our discharge, except a few who sailed up the coast to San Francisco. Ten were chosen, including myself, to act as pioneers, one of whom was to act as the Captain over the nine. That was Elisha Everett. We hardly knew what way to strike out, for we had no guide, except an old California map with very few rivers or anything else marked on it, and a paper pretending to give the route, that somebody had given to some of our men.

On the twenty-first day of July we made a move for home, it being just one year since we took up our line of march at Council Bluffs. Our course was up the San Pedro,[6] the pioneers leading out. Made that day about ten miles and made an early encampment on the bank of the river. On the twenty-second the pioneers led out, leaving the San Pedro, bearing to our right in a northern

---

4. The Los Angeles River.

5. In the version written for Hittell he says in retrospect under the twentieth, "for the journey to Salt Lake." But in the Huntington version he records under the nineteenth, "prepare for a general move home, that is, to hunt for the main body of the Church," and in the Utah version he says under the twentieth, "going home (and where that was, no one in camp knows where that was)."

That the Mormons were not sure at that time of the identity of Bear River Valley is shown in Bigler's as well as the other diaries. Standage under June 29 records "Bear River Valley or any other destined place in California," and Bliss says on July 22 in San Fernando that "we bought our canteens full of wine as we expect to get no more till we arrive at Bear Valley." It is possible that Bigler might have thought, at least in the older versions, of Bear Valley in California. See also footnote 19 of section iv.

6. Los Angeles River.

course over a sandy plain some twelve miles to a Spanish ranch. I think it was called Picoes.[7] Here the pioneers halted and got some wine to drink and pears to eat. After going about one and a half miles further towards the mountain we camped. The company behind was late getting up to camp. Here our company bought two horses, one of a Spaniard, the other of an Indian, the two for sixteen dollars (high).

On the twenty-third we continued our journey northward crossing a mountain, and in ascending the mountain our road led up a narrow point, and so abrupt and steep on either side that if a horse made one false step, he would be precipitated for one hundred fifty feet or more. To my surprise I saw a Spanish cart track where Spaniards had crossed the mountain with a cart. After crossing the mountain about three miles, we encamped on a small rivulet. Here I cut the initials of my name on a young sycamore tree that we camped under. An Indian family traveled with us today.

On the twenty-fourth we continued down this stream about a mile when we came to an open valley about five miles wide. We travelled across the plain and about 11:00 A.M. we stopped and camped on the north side of what we called Santa Clara River. Here was a ranch. I think it was called San Fernando ranch.[8] Here the pioneers stopped until all the company got up and held a consultation whether it would not be well to purchase some beef cattle and drive them along for beef.

July 25. In camp all day; it being Sunday.

July 26. Captain Everett and a few others went to see the *Alcalde* [9] to learn what we could buy a few beef cattle

7. San Fernando Mission. Called Pico's Rancho because Andrés Pico was lessee of a part of the secularized mission property.
8. It was the San Francisco ranch.
9. Ignacio del Valle, owner of San Francisco ranch.

for, and reported on their return that we could get them for six dollars per head. On the twenty-seventh we purchased forty-five nice three-year olds, and on the twenty-eighth we made a general move driving our cattle, and in crossing a lofty and rather brushy mountain we lost fifteen head! We found them to be very wild. They would charge upon us while we were on our horses endeavoring to drive them.

On the twenty-ninth we crossed a high mountain with a very bad road losing three more of our cattle, and on the thirtieth the camp concluded to stop a while and kill and jerk our meat. Our Indian guide says here used to be a boiling spring.

July 31. The camp was up all last night drying meat. There was plenty wood handy, and fires and scaffolds were made. All hands busy taking care of our beef except the pioneers, who set out this morning, leaving the camp behind to spend the day in drying meat. We went about fifteen miles and camped in a canyon on a small stream. Here we found cut on a tree the name, "Peter Lebeck who was killed by a Bear Oct. 17, 1837." [10]

August 1. The next morning we continued down the rivulet about three miles when we entered a wide valley. We travelled across about ten miles when we came to a

10. At the present town of Lebec in Grapevine Canyon. This and Bliss's entry under the same date are the first recordings of the mysterious inscription. Both the Bancroft and Huntington versions spell the name correctly, Lebeck; the next recorder of the landmark, William P. Blake of the Pacific Railroad Survey in 1853, misspells the name Le Beck; and the Hittell and Utah version use this misspelling likewise. It was further corrupted into Pierre Lebeque and emerged finally as Lebec when a hotel and a post office were established at the place. The piece of bark which Bigler mentions in the Utah version was cut out in 1889 and is now in the Kern County Museum in Bakersfield. This bark and the statements by the two Mormons should induce the people of Kern County to rectify their spelling of the name of the unknown pioneer.

lake. The guide said it would swim our animals. Here our guide left us. Today we saw large herds of antelope, and the mosquitoes about this lake were awful bad.

August 2. This morning Captain Everett went to hunt up an Indian to pilot us farther on our way, while we remained in camp, and at 2:00 P.M. the rear part of our camp got up, when we made a move about six miles and camped for the night. The water was not good (alkali). According to our map we had with us, we believed this to be Tulare Lake.

The next morning Captain Everett returned with a guide and seven other Indians. The guide says we will have to keep up on this side (east) of the lake about twenty miles and then cross a river. We made about twelve miles and camped on the bank of the river, and we called it Tulare River (but at present I have my doubts. I think this lake was Kern Lake and this river Kern River).[11] The river runs swift and seemed to abound with plenty of fish. Elk and antelope seemed to be very plentiful along here.

On the fourth of August we traveled up the river some six or eight miles and crossed by swimming our animals, and we made a raft and ferried the most of our luggage over. Some waded and carried their things on their heads.

August 5. This morning our guide left us because we would not hire the whole of them (eight in number). Here we left this great valley to our left, traveling over hills and over a high mountain, and encamped in the canyon of the mountain, making some twenty-five miles. Here water was scarce and we were all night watering our animals.

---

11. Bigler is right. It was Kern Lake, now long disappeared. The correction is lacking in the Huntington version and seems to allow the conclusion that it is older than the Bancroft version.

August 6. Made about ten miles and encamped in a canyon near some Indian lodges.[12]

August 7. This morning a horse was missing—either got away or stolen by Indians. Made that day about fifteen miles over hills and encamped on a creek nearly dry, the water standing in holes.

August 8. We went about six miles and came to a beautiful creek about twenty yards wide. Here we sent to an Indian village close by to get a guide. Several Indians came and two proffered to go with us two days. They did not appear to know much about the country.

August 9. Made about twenty-five miles and encamped on a beautiful little river. The natives came into camp. They told us they believed we were good people and they would not steal our horses. The road today was good.

August 10. This morning we made a raft to carry our things across and swam our horses. We then traveled west, passing through an Indian settlement where they have large quantities of fish and roots out to dry. We made that day about eight miles and camped in a heavy grove of oak timber near a slough.

August 11. Today we made about twenty-eight miles north and encamped in a grove on the banks of a river near an Indian village. We had no guide today. The day was extremely warm, and many suffered for want of water and gave out by the way. As soon as the pioneers reached the river they filled their canteens and sent them back, and as fast as the company reached the river, their canteens were taken and filled and sent back to their comrades, and thus the sufferers were relieved.

---

12. The officers called a meeting and admonished "that the brethren should harken to their officers and to those appointed to command etc. and to be diligent in keeping the commandments of God. We have had several prayer meetings since leaving Los Angeles" (Huntington). In the Utah version this meeting is recorded under August 7.

January 1848   1.75

Thur 13th Clear as a bell and the water is a falling and the Mill safe

" 14th Clear & fine Sat " 15th Clear

Sun 16th Clear and warm this Morning My self and Br. Brown went to look for our horses the grass has growed fine the mansanetta and the alder is in Bloom .

Sun " 23d Clear this day Myself and 4 others mooved in to a house that we had built last week Mr Wemers wife who was hired to Cook for us and But on Christmas Morning just at day light we was cald to

29-P3

FACSIMILE PAGE FROM BIGLER'S DIARY

174¹ Jan. 1848

Breakfast; we was washing our
faces we was cald the second time
before we was ready to obey. She
told us plainly that she was Boss
and that we must cum at the first
call which we had alwais had before ^done^

On Christmas morning in bed she swore
ᵒ That she would cook for us no more
ᵒ Unless wᵈ cum at the first call
ᵒ For I am mistress of you all.

This we did not like and we Revolted
from under hur government
She was partial in hur cooking
She had some favorites and would
always keep back the best part of
the vituals

——— Monday 24ᵗʰ this day
some kind of mettle was

FACSIMILE PAGE FROM BIGLER'S DIARY

was found in the tail race that
that looks like goald first discov
ered by James Martial, the Bos of the mill.
Sunday 30 clear & has been
all the last week our metal
has been tride and prooves to
be Goald it is thought to be
rich we have pict up more than
a hundred dollars woth last
one week

February. 1848

Sun 6th the wether has been clean
and warm the past week to day
my self & Mr. Bargen went
up over the creek to look for
goald I found 6 B dollars wo
Saturday 12th this afternoon
I did not work being tired
not verry well I took the
gun & went a long down
the creek to hunt for ducks

FACSIMILE PAGE FROM BIGLER'S DIARY

17 Feb 18__

but in reality to look for gole
a bout a half a mile down the
Creek I discovered some Rock on
the oposite side that indicated
that gold was thare I soon took
off my shirt & pants and crost over
I soon pict up $1,50 cts worth living
in the seems of the rocks.
but what is the worst of all
it is on Capt Sutters and Mr
Martials land for after the
goald was found in the mill tail
they leased a large scope of land
of the Indians for 3 years and have sent
to the governor at Monteray to have it secured
so I cannot have any claim on it
Sunday 13 Rains most all day
I spent the day in looking
for goale I found $8=00 cts
worth
Monday 14th Rainy we did not
work on the mill I spent

FACSIMILE PAGE FROM BIGLER'S DIARY

The next day we laid by, while Captain Everett and a few pioneers went up the river to examine the route, as we were near the mouth of the canyon where the river came out of the mountain. From the map and the paper we had brought with us from Los Angeles, our intention was to find a pass and cross the mountain. There was talk of Walkers Pass, but where that was we could not find out from the chart we had, and the Indians did not seem to know anything about it. In the evening the camp got word to move up the river about ten miles. Captain Everett did not return.

The next day we moved up and late in the evening the Captain returned and reported that in his opinion we could not cross the mountain. He and his men had been up the river to where they could not go any farther with their animals and he saw no chance. The mountain ledges came so close to the river and so steep and rough that to him it seemed impossible to travel up the river with our animals. I believe this river was thought to be Kings River. A meeting was now called of the whole camp what to do. It was decided that we turn back and take Fremont's route for Sutter's Fort.[13]

Accordingly the next morning we went back about four miles where we crossed the river and traveled about six miles and camped. Many of the camp went in and bathed. We were visited by several of the natives who sang and danced in their style, which was quite amusing.

On the sixteenth we traveled a northwest course without a pilot and camped on a beautiful river about one hundred

---

13. They were east of modern Fresno now; the impassable canyon is Kings Canyon. The map they had was doubtless the Frémont-Preuss map, on which Walkers Pass, which is much farther south, is not recorded. The "beautiful little river" they crossed on the tenth must have been the Kaweah.

yards wide.[14] The current was strong. The country over which we traveled was rich and loose.

On the seventeenth traveled northwest fifteen miles and camped on a river, but it was dry. We had to dig in the sand for water.

August 18. Made about twenty-five miles and camped on a river that was nearly dry. Here we saw lots of antelope and some elk.

August 19. Made about twenty-five miles and encamped on a beautiful river about one hundred yards wide. Supposed to be the San Joaquin.[15] Here we were visited by some Indians who traded us some young corn and melons.

August 20. This morning we crossed the river and traveled in a northwestern direction a few miles, then crossed another river about seventy yards wide; thence west for five miles down the river and at 3:00 P.M. camped. Here we were again visited by some Indians to trade. The chief had a paper given to him by some Americans saying that he was a good Indian and his men would not steal. Made today about twenty-two miles.

The next day we continued down the river passing through the Indian village. They had some nice corn patches and part of it topped, and the ears of corn could be seen hanging on the stalks. It reminded me of home and had the appearance of fall season of the year at home, and in spite of me, a feeling of home strongly crept over me. We traveled down this river for about ten miles and camped on the Merced River.[16] Here the natives brought us corn and melons to sell. We learned from them that some Americans have settled down this river about nine miles. We think they may be Mormons who have come around

14. The San Joaquin River.
15. The Merced River.
16. The Stanislaus (or the Tuolumne) River.

the Horn in the ship *Brooklyn* last season.[17] Captain [Andrew] Lytle and two others set out to go and see who they are.

On the evening of the twenty-first of August a council was held by the camp what was best to do in regard to fitting out a few of the boys who had started with us and were short of the necessary outfit to carry them through to where we might find our friends in the valleys of the mountains. It was decided that four men go ahead to Sutter's Fort and see Captain Sutter and ascertain what he had to sell and how much meal, corn, wheat and flour, horses and mules etc., with their prices, so that we might know what we were able to do in fitting out those who were short, and also to replenish our own stock of provision.

August 22. Traveled about twenty miles over bad road and over low mountains and through brush. Halted at an Indian settlement. Bought a few watermelons and some corn.

On the twenty-third we made about eighteen or twenty miles over rough road and past a few Indian huts. The men were away. The squaws and children on our approach ran for life. They thought surely they were going to be taken. At 3:00 P.M. we camped on a creek with a few holes of water, the grass not plenty, being burned by the Indians.

On the twenty-fourth traveled northwest some eighteen miles and encamped on a river. I think we called it the Macogamy.[18] Here a few American families were living.

17. The reference is to Brannan's New Hope settlement. However, there were other Mormons scattered in the Delta district. Jones (p. 18) mentioned on June 11, that his camp was visited by a "brother" named "Rhodes." Thomas Rhoads had come with the great migration of 1846 and had settled on the Cosumnes. Here the detachment learned that Brigham Young had selected the Great Salt Lake Valley as the future colony of the Saints.

18. The Cosumnes (or the Mokelumne) River.

I think their names were Murphys.[19] Still I am not sure. It did our eyes good to see them, the women and children, also chickens and milk cows, and the large piles of wheat already thrashed and cleaned for the sack. It was said there was over two thousand bushels. Here it was where we heard for the first time where the Church was. We were told that Brigham Young and the Twelves with three hundred pioneers had arrived at the Great Salt Lake and that five hundred wagons were close behind. Late in the evening Captain Lytle, who had left on the twenty-first returned, and reported that some of the people he visited were Mormons.

August 25. This morning we got a few bushels wheat for one dollar per bushel. The Spanish phrase and price was two dollars per *fanega*. Our course today was northwest across a large plain for twenty miles and we encamped on the north side of the American River about one mile and half from Sutter's Fort.

August 26. Laid by while some visited the Fort, where there was a blacksmith's shop, and got their animals shod, as some of them were tender footed. The price of shoeing was one dollar for each shoe made and nailed on. We learned here was plenty of grain and unbolted flour and peas to be had. Unbolted flour (which was all the kind in California those days) was worth eight dollars per sack, peas one dollar and half per bushel. Captain Sutter seemed to have plenty of everything in the shape of cattle, horses and mules, grain etc. Several of our boys concluded to stop here and go to work for Sutter, as he was wanting to hire and was offering pretty fair wages, as the boys thought, and fit themselves up and come on the next spring.[20]

19. Martin Murphy Jr., one of the Murphys who had come to California in 1844 with the Stevens-Murphy-Townsend Party.

20. According to the Hittell and Utah versions Sutter offered twenty-five to forty dollars a month.

On the twenty-seventh the pioneers struck out leaving behind the greater part of the camp, who expected to stop another day and more fully complete their outfit for the journey. At 2:00 P.M. we camped, making about eighteen miles in a northeast direction.

On the twenty-eighth we made about the same distance and camped on Bear River. Here were a few families, [one] by the name of Johnson.[21]

August 29. Rained in the night, the first we have had for some time. Our course today was east over low mountains and we camped in a canyon. The country began to be covered with oak and pine timber.

August 30. It thundered and threatened rain all day. Made fifteen miles and camped under a nice cluster of pine trees, plenty of water and the best of grass.

August 31. Today we passed over some high mountains but not rough. The road for a pack trail was good. We encamped on the top of a mountain by a cold spring, making about eighteen miles.

September 1. Went ten miles and halted for dinner while Captain Everett and a few of his men went ahead to examine the road, as it began to grow rough and rocky. Here the camp found a large patch of thimble berries, which afforded the camp an excellent feast. In an hour or so the Captain returned and reported that there was a nice little valley about two miles ahead with plenty of grass, but some of the way to this valley was rocky and bad. We made [it] and camped, making about twelve miles. We passed an emigrant wagon. It was broken to pieces. We gave this place the name of Bear Valley because we saw lots of bear signs in it. The valley was rich, pea vines as high as a man's head, and the bears had tramped and made roads in all directions. The place was

---

21. The easternmost outpost of northern California, settled by an American, a German, and two Frenchmen.

surrounded with high mountains. Pine timber as thick as it could stand, and many from eight to ten feet in diameter and more than two hundred feet high. Here we found two more wagons and chains. There had been a temporary blacksmith forge.

September 2. Laid by to let our animals feed, as it was extra good feed. I took my gun and left camp to hunt a few hours, but soon gave it up in consequence of its being so hard traveling over rocks, I seated myself on a high rock at the north end of the valley, where I had a full view of a mountain, still north of me about half a mile distant to me. It was a sight to look upon. I think the mountain must have been a mile high and appeared to be a solid mass of rocks, with here and there a few scattered pines. It looked grand and yet lonesome and dismal.

September 3. At seven this morning we were on the move, traveled up a high steep mountain a little southeast of camp and through a low place or valley, thence a little north of east over mountains and on the summit of one of those mountains we passed near a small lake or pond. Here one of our men shot at a deer but did not get it. We made an early encampment on a creek running west. We passed a wagon that looked lonesome and truly forsaken. There were some old clothes and tin pans in it, which seemed rather to prove that there were no Indians in the mountains. Near our camp we found a grave and on the headboard was the name Smith, died Oct. 7, 1846.[22] We were now surrounded with high mountains covered with a heavy forest of pine and balsam timber. The land looked dark and dreary, and I thought if there were any witches and hobgoblins in the world, they must live in these mountains.

---

22. James A. Smith in Bliss. Not the James Smith of the Donner Party, but one who must have crossed the summit about the same time as Lienhard.

On the fourth we traveled up a high mountain and around the highest peaks between two lakes, indeed, we passed several of them today on the very tops of the mountains, and some of the company said they had fish in them. At 2:00 P.M. we camped on top of a mountain by one of the coldest springs I ever saw. We traveled slow in order that the company left at Sutter's may overtake us.

September 5. At about seven we were on the march passing through a nice little valley two or three miles long and about three-fourths of a mile wide. We ascended the mountain passing over snow three feet deep. We now had gained the summit and main chain of the great Sierra Nevada mountains, and on the east side at the top was a windlass, where emigrants had to haul up their wagons over a very steep ascent in order to gain the summit of the great Sierra Nevada. Passing down the mountain to the head of Truckee River some six or eight miles, we came to a shanty built last winter, and about this cabin we found the skeletons of several human beings.[23] I discovered a hand. It was nearly entire. It had been partly burned to a crisp. The little finger was not burnt. The flesh seemed to be a little dried. I judged it to be the hand of a woman. I do not believe the wolves disturbed them. The place had the appearance that they had been burned after death. Some of our company thought that the Indians found them in their starving and helpless condition and had killed and burned them. Others did not believe it from the fact that we had passed several wagons with

23. They had come upon the Lake camp of the Donner Party, where the Schallenberger and Graves shanties had not been burned; nor had the gruesome remnants been buried as ordered by General Kearny on his return march on June 22, 1847. "Apparently Major Swords or his detail shirked the labor, so that many bones and fragments remained to the horror of later passers-by. They did not, moreover, burn all the cabins" (Stewart, p. 277). See the entry in Jones under the date of June 22.

trunks and boxes and clothing all scattered about and around the wagons. That if Indians had been about they would have carried off the clothing and light trunks for their own particular use. I noticed the timber about this shanty that had been cut down; the stumps were ten or twelve feet high. This showed how deep the snow was at the time it was cut. After leaving this painful looking place about three miles, we camped in a handsome little valley by a creek, where good water and grass was plenty.

VI.

THE RETURN TO
SUTTER'S FORT: 1847-1848

Bigler's detachment was now near Donner Lake, and they could hope to reach Salt Lake before the end of the fall. But here fate intervened again. On September 6, Bigler and his party met Sam Brannan on his way back to San Francisco after his fruitless effort to induce Brigham Young and the mass of the Saints to erect their new Zion in California.

Brannan, after inspecting the New Hope Farm, had left Sutter's Fort on April 26, 1847, and arrived after a ride of less than forty days at Fort Hall in June.[1] Here he found a communication from Brigham Young which informed him that by June 6, Brigham Young and his pioneer company had reached Bitter Creek, thirty miles west of Laramie; and that the Mormons would not go to the west coast at present because they had not the means.

---

1. In present-day Idaho. The important station on the northern route to Oregon and California.

In fact, Brigham Young had already decided on the (
Salt Lake Valley, scorned by many, but praised by so
On the thirtieth of June, Brannan met Brigham on ine
banks of the Green River, somewhere near the mouth of
the Big Sandy.

Here the great discussion took place which was to decide the future of the Mormon Church.[3] Brannan, a born
salesman, seemed to have all the trumps in his hands: the
Latter-day Saints had been well received in San Diego,
Los Angeles, and Yerba Buena. In the latter city they
formed a substantial part of the population, and Sam
Brannan was already a civic leader and owner of a printing press and a newspaper. New Hope was a flourishing
colony. Everything was ready to receive several thousands
of Saints and make California a Mormon colony.

Brigham Young, however, had decided in favor of Salt
Lake Valley and could not be taken in by the smooth-
tongued Brannan. On the contrary, the enthusiasm of
the elder from San Francisco had a decidedly cooling effect upon the successor of the prophet. Logical argument
and factual realism could not touch Brigham Young. He
believed in the Lord, and wherever the Mormons would
break the soil the Lord would give his blessings.[4]

While the negotiations were still going on in the camp

2. Heinrich Lienhard, himself afterward anti-Mormon, passed here
eleven months before with a few Mormons in advance of the Church. He
wrote: "The soil is deep, rich, black, and mixed with sand, and is doubtless potentially highly productive. The clear sky-blue surface of the
lake, the warm sunny atmosphere, the high mountains with the beautiful
countryside at their base, through which we were traveling on a fine
road—all this put me in a very happy mood. All day long I felt like
singing and whistling; and if there had been a single white family there,
I believe I would have stayed. What a pity that the magnificent countryside was uninhabited" (Lienhard, p. 103).

3. The dramatic events of the following days have been recorded repeatedly, best perhaps by Bailey in *Sam Brannan* pp. 99 ff.

4. Brigham Young had decided to settle in the "neighborhood of the
Rocky Mountains" before January 20, 1846. See the "Circular of the
High Council" from *Journal History* printed in Golder, pp. 71 ff.

on Green River, another chance turned up for Sam Brannan to sell California to the Mormons. As mentioned above, on the march to Santa Fe the Battalion had left the sick and weak members and doubtless some unwilling stragglers in Pueblo on the Arkansas. They were under the command of Captain James Brown.[5] This detachment had decided to march to California via the Fort Hall route for their discharge and back pay. On the fourth of July a dozen soldiers of this detachment, in pursuit of horse thieves, accidentally came into the camp where Young and Brannan had not yet finished bickering about California and Utah. Learning that the company from Pueblo was already on the march west, the president ordered the leader of the platoon that had been sent to find the stolen horses, Sergeant Thomas Williams, to betake himself with Sam Brannan to meet and pilot the detachment of former invalids to California, where Brannan would help them get their discharge and back pay. Brannan was delighted, of course. The Mormons from Pueblo numbered more than a hundred, and once in California, they might act as a magnet to the rest.

But this plan came to naught, too. Brannan and Williams had not gone far beyond South Pass when they met Brown and his company. Together, on July 29, they arrived at the camp in Salt Lake Valley only a few days after the pioneers. To Brannan's dismay Brigham Young had lost no time in laying out what was to become Salt Lake City and to start preparations to sow the first crop.

But worse was in store for poor Sam. The invalid company was to remain in the new settlement, and only Captain Brown with a small escort was to go back to California to settle the affairs of the Battalion. To add insult to injury, not Brannan but Brown was entrusted with the

5. See Bigler's entries of October 15 and November 11, 1846, and footnote 18, section iii.

76

epistle to Captain Jefferson Hunt and the letter for the Bigler detachment.

Brannan must have left New Zion in black rage. He remained a Mormon as long as it was in his interest, but he grew estranged from the faith, especially after the discovery of gold. From the standpoint of the Church, Brigham Young's determination to make the little attractive Utah the center of the Church of the Latter-day Saints was doubtless a wise one regardless of what the Lord might have had to do with his choice. The discovery of gold and the subsequent developments would doubtless have smashed the organization of the Church in California like a lighter against a golden rock.

Sam Brannan never saw Brigham Young or Salt Lake City again. Yet he remained a leader of the Church in California for some time. New Hope was liquidated, and no attempt was made to establish another agricultural community within the orbit of San Francisco. Yet Sam continued to preach and collect money for the Church. After the discovery of gold he made a bold attempt to get from the Mormon miners a tithe for the Church and a cut for himself, as Bigler and others narrate. With the founding of the Mormon colony of San Bernardino in 1851, or with several similar attempts, Sam had no connection. When he was asked to turn over to the Lord the money he owed the Church and the tithings he was supposed to have collected, he is said to have replied, "Give me a receipt signed by the Lord and you will get your money"—an often repeated and probably fictitious story although quite in harmony with Brannan's personality.

September 6. Soon after leaving camp this morning, we met Sam Brannan, who had been up to Salt Lake to meet our emigration. He informed us that Captain Brown with his detachment from the Pueblo country on the Arkansas was just behind on his way to Monterey to get their discharge,[6] and that the Captain had a package of letters and also an epistle from Brigham Young and the Twelve to the Battalion boys. As part of our Company was still behind and had not as yet overtaken the pioneers since leaving the settlements, we concluded to turn back to our last camping place and there await the arrival of Captain Brown, and also for the rear part of our company, where all might be together and all hear the news together. After we had returned to camp, Brannan stopped an hour or so to let his animal feed and to eat a bite himself and talk with the boys etc. He was traveling alone. He and Captain Brown had had a quarrel that morning (as I understood), and so sharp had words and threats been made that Brannan left the Captain and his crowd to travel without his company. Mr. Brannan gave us a glowing account of the great Salt Lake and the country with its surroundings.[7]

September 7. Late this afternoon the camp was all up, and Captain Brown had also arrived. Nearly every man got a letter either from his family or friend, and truly we had a season of rejoicing together in the mountains, although a few had news of sadness. They had either lost a loving wife or a child or parent since last they saw or heard from them.

The epistle was to the effect that all who had no families and those who had and did not expect to meet them at the Great Salt Lake before the next season and had not plenty of provision with them to last until the coming harvest: it

6. As stated, the Pueblo detachment had been held back at the Salt Lake. Only a few men made the trip with Brannan and Brown.

7. "Glowing account" is obviously a mistake by the chronicler; perhaps he wanted to say "gloomy." In the Hittell and Utah versions he records that Brannan told them the Salt Lake country was no place for the Mormons to settle. All other accounts agree with this, except one: Stanley ("Sutter's Mormon Workmen," p. 281) asserts that Bigler actually said "glowing" and that Hittell changed it maliciously.

would be wisdom for all such to return to California and go to work and fit themselves out with plenty of clothing, stock, provision, etc. and come up the next season to the valley. One hundred and forty-three pioneers had arrived and had not much provision with them, and they had already sent out a hunting party to kill buffalo and that provision at Fort Hall was scarce and very high.

While we were at this camp, some of our boys went out hunting and when they came in reported they had found a shanty with the dead lying about it undisturbed by wild beasts. The flesh seemed to be completely dried on their bones. There were men, women, and children. Some of them were cut up having their arms and legs cut off, others their ribs sawn from the back bones, while some had their skulls sawed open and the brains taken out! [8]

I understood they were Missourians emigrating last season to California, about ninety souls. They became short of grub and had fallen out among themselves and became divided; the able and strong pushed forward and reached the settlements, and before help could be sent back, a heavy snow storm had overtaken the companies left in the mountains; and even when help did reach them very few were found alive. Children seemed to endure starvation better than adults. We were told at Sutter's Fort that children were saved but not till after they had eaten of their dead parents. There was one man at Sutter's [at the time] we came along, whom some of our boys said they saw. They were told that he was found with a box full of arms and legs that he had to live on, and it was thought by some at the Fort that he had killed a woman and boxed her up to eat. [9]

---

8. Bigler's companions had come across the camp of the Donner families at Prosser Creek.

9. The definitive account of the tragedy is George Stewart's *Ordeal by Hunger.*

September 8. This morning myself and some thirty others gave our brethren the parting hand, but not till after we had divided our provision with them, barely keeping enough to last us back to the first settlement, about one hundred and fifty miles.[10]

On the eleventh as we were returning, we found a little grave opened. The coffin or box was broken open. The child eaten up no doubt by wild beasts, the skull lying close by. The pillow, that was under its head, was there, partly torn up. Near this place we found a grave, and on the tombstone the name of Ann West, aged sixty-two years.[11] That same day we passed by the grave of Henry Hoyt.[12] He was one of our Battalion boys in the rear part of our company and died in crossing these mountains; as the pioneers were two days in advance and had all the tools for digging with them, the rear had nothing except a hatchet or two to dig his grave with. He was buried on the side of the mountain high up under a low spreading oak and so shallow that the air could get to him and it smelled bad.

On the twelfth, we reached Johnson's, where we got a little flour and a few peas.[13]

On the fourteenth, at 1:00 P.M., we reached our old camp ground near Mr. Sutter's. After eating a bite of dinner we sent three men to see Captain Sutter. Late in the evening they returned reporting they had seen Mr.

10. In the Huntington version the parting is told more dramatically: "It was hard to part but we knew the Council of the President and the Twelve was wise and we would be safe in obeying it." The story of the party continuing their trip to the Salt Lake is told in the journal of Robert S. Bliss.

11. The wife of Thomas West, who had traveled with Edwin Bryant in 1846.

12. Henry P. Hoyt had left Sutter's Fort with the rear detachment on August 29.

13. The entries from September 15, 1847, to April 11, 1848, are lacking in the Huntington version.

Sutter, and he was willing to give the whole of us employment. He would either hire us by the month or by the job. He was intending to build a mill and wanted mill timbers got out and a race cut about three miles long. He would pay twenty-five dollars per month for working on the race or he would give twelve and one-half cents a yard. We talked the thing over among ourselves that night and the next morning we closed a bargain with him to work on the race for twelve and one-half cents per yard to be paid in cash. He was to board us, but we were to do our own cooking.[14]

The same day we concluded our bargain with Sutter we moved on to the ground some six miles east of his Fort where there was an adobe building handy to our work, and [it] answered first rate to quarter in. He also gave us the privilege of letting our animals run with his "Cavaather" [15] or band of horses gratuitously. This we felt was very kind. He had a large band herded by some vaqueros or Indians, who were also overseen by a white man who had the band brought up every night and corralled.

On the seventeenth all hands were on the ditch with spades, plows, picks, shovels, and a few scrapers, Sutter furnishing all the tools. Our teams to work on the race were oxen, Spanish cattle that we had gotten from Sutter as part pay. Some of them were not very well broken, and some had never seen a yoke nor anything else, I was going to say unless it was a "greaser." However, the boys soon got them so as to manage them with very little trouble.

I continued to labor on the ditch until Monday the twenty-seventh of September, when a man dressed in buckskin came to our quarters while we were at dinner, inform-

---

14. They were hired to build the grist or flour mill in Natoma, at the site of Brighton.
15. *Caballada.*

ing us that Captain Sutter wanted four men from our crowd to go with him (the man in buckskin) up the American fork into the mountains about thirty miles, to work and help build a sawmill. This man, whom we were to accompany, was James W. Marshall, an entire stranger to us, but proved to be a gentleman nevertheless. He told us that he had been up in the mountains with a few hands only a short time; but as some of them were going to leave soon he wished to get a few more. We learned that he and Sutter were in copartnership in building the sawmill. So late that afternoon myself and three others set out with Mr. Marshall, accompanied by a Charles Bennett late from Oregon.[16] Marshall taking at the same time an ox team and wagon loaded with provisions and a few tools.

We arrived on the twenty-ninth. Here I found several of the Battalion boys at work who had remained at Sutter's at the time our company passed there in August. Four, however, soon left and returned to the Fort and went to work on Sutter's flouring mill. The country around the mill site looked wild and lonesome.[17] Surrounded by high mountains on the south side of the river, the mountains were densely covered with pine, balsam, pinion pine, redwood, white oak, and low down the live oak, while on the north side there was not so much timber; the mountains were more abrupt and rocky, covered in places with patches of chamisal and greasewood. The country was infested by wolves, grizzly bears, and Indians. The work now to be done was to get out mill timbers, dig out a mill site, put in a dam, and cut a tail race forty or fifty rods long.

---

16. The other three were Mormons and Battalion boys: Israel Evans, Azariah Smith, William Johnson (Hittell).

17. The place was called Culuma, later Coloma, after a Maidu village there. Bancroft, *History*, VI, 27, and other American romanticists have given the meaning as "beautiful vale."

SUTTER'S FORT FROM *Century Illustrated Monthly Magazine* (1891)

PHOTOGRAPH BY COURTESY OF BANCROFT LIBRARY

DONNER LAKE   FROM A WATER COLOR BY EDWARD VISCHER IN BANCROFT LIBRARY

They had already built a nice double log cabin with a hall or entry between. The building was built of nice pine logs and covered with pine clapboards, riven out with a frow, bastard fashion as they called it. The house was built by a spring gulch on the side of the mountain about one-fourth, or nearly so, of a mile from the mill site. A family by the name of Wimmer [18] lived in the west end, while the other was used by the hired men to sleep in. Wimmer's wife was doing the cooking for the hands while Wimmer himself oversaw the Indians (eight in number), showing them how to work. On the night of the third of October we were aroused by our tame Indians, who said there were bad Indians around. They [the wild Indians] would not speak when spoken to or tell what they wanted, and the next night we were disturbed and aroused again by the words, "Malo hinty, malo hinty," from our Indians, which meant bad Indian, bad Indian. We could see nothing but we could hear them walk. Our Indians said they saw some of them, and some of our party caught a glimpse of an Indian. We could not get them to talk. They kept at a proper distance in the dark among the pine timber. Up to this time we had not thought of much danger, and we began to think we had been rather careless. There were ten white men and only four guns. We (the Mormon boys) had left our muskets below, and for the guns present there were scarcely any balls. All was in a bustle. Some commenced forthwith to molding bullets, others to cleaning and putting in order the guns, for some of them were in poor trim for an action. For the first time we set out a guard, and we kept it up too for some time to come, when they seemed to have left entirely, finding out perhaps that

18. Peter Wimmer and his family had come to California with Lienhard in 1846. Lienhard, as well as Bigler and Marshall, spell the name Weimer (or Wemer). This was perhaps the original form. The family was generally called Wimmer and later accepted this spelling.

we had something else besides bows and arrows for them.

Our grub was mainly unbolted flour, pork, mutton, salmon, peas, tea, coffee, and sugar. Sometimes when Sutter failed to send up supplies, we became short of meat, and to remedy this, Mr. Marshall chose me to be his hunter and frequently sent me out with his rifle (and he had a good one) to kill a deer, as they were plenty, and [with] an Indian to carry it in. This kind of labor I had no particular objections to and would not have grumbled in the least if Marshall had continued to keep it up. By New Year's we had the mill frame up and the fore bay in and ditch dug for the tail race, but it was found not to be deep enough and we had already struck the base rock (granite). This was rather a drawback as it was now going to be a slow job to cut it out deep enough. The dam was nearly completed. We had built it of brush laid in with the butts downstream, but it commenced to rain and continued for several days. The river rose, fears were entertained that all our work would be lost, and Marshall with his men worked in the rain almost night and day to save the dam and mill. By the middle of January the weather became settled, and the river on the fall and everything saved. About this time an altercation had taken place between Wimmer's family and some of the mill hands and they (the hands) had built a snug little cabin near the mill and were living in it, doing their own cooking.[19]

---

19. A delightful entry explaining the cause of the altercation with Mrs. Wimmer is omitted from the Bancroft and Hittell versions, but is preserved in the fragment of the Pioneer Society and printed in the Utah version under date of January 23. It accuses Jennie Wimmer of being partial with her distribution of food and indicates that she took offense when the boys did not come at her first call for Christmas breakfast:

On Christmas morn in bed she swore
That she would cook for us no more,
Unless we'd come at the first call,
For I am mistress of you all.

Right here I will give the names of the men at work on the sawmill at that time: Peter L. Wimmer, Charles Bennett, William Scott, (since then Scott committed suicide by cutting his throat!) Alexander Stevens, James S. Brown, James Barger, William Johnson, Azariah Smith, and myself; the last mentioned six were Mormons. There had been other men at work but had left soon after I came to the sawmill and were at work on the lower mill near the Fort.[20] Their names were Ira Willis, Sidney Willis (two brothers) and William Kountze (Battalion boys).

Everything was now going on nicely, Bennett and Scott working at the bench, Stevens hewing timbers, Brown and Barger either chopping, scoring, or chopping down timber. Sometimes the two latter whipsawed, and sometimes it was Brown and an Indian that sawed together. [The latter] seemed to be very fond and anxious to learn, and when we told him we were making a mill that would saw by itself, he did not believe it. Said it was a damned lie, such a thing in his estimation could not be done. Wimmer had charge of some Indians cutting the race a little deeper. I was drilling into some boulders near where the water wheel was to be, while Marshall superintended the whole affair. He was in the habit of visiting Wimmer and the Indians every afternoon to see how they were making it in the granite, which proved the most of it to be soft and rotten.

20. The grist mill at Natoma.

VII.

THE FATEFUL TWENTY-FOURTH OF JANUARY: 1848

Bigler's participation in the discovery of gold at Sutter's Mill is the most dramatic phase of his career, and his chronicle of this event is historically his most valuable contribution to those decisive years. Bigler's diary is the one and only source which gives a direct eyewitness account of the happenings on the twenty-fourth of January, 1848, and the following days. Another Mormon present at the mill on that day, Azariah Smith, kept a somewhat sketchy diary; all other accounts of the discovery are based on hearsay or on recollection. In later years Bigler added details from recollection, and for this reason some historians have brushed aside Bigler's account as "reminiscent testimony," and they maintain that his "statement must be taken with caution." In view of this circumstance some interpolation is necessary to realize my hope that the publication of the Bigler journals will put an end to the more than a century old controversy concerning the fateful weeks of January and February, 1848.

The Bigler diaries from June, 1846, to September, 1848, have stood the test of rigorous examination. Not a single instance could be discovered where Bigler deviates from the truth for personal or religious or political reasons. The very few instances marked in the footnotes, where Bigler's statements may be open to question, are of no importance and allow not the slightest doubt of the

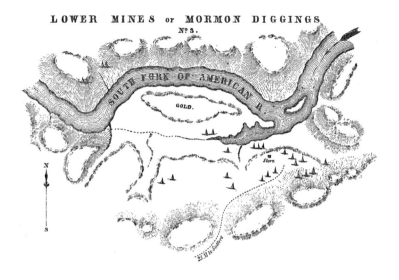

LOWER MINES or MORMON DIGGINGS

veracity and meticulosity of Bigler as a chronicler. No
other sources relating to the discovery of gold have stood
this test. Here, then, is Bigler's account:

My journal tells me it was on the afternoon [1] of the
twenty-fourth day of January, 1848, while I was at my
drill busy preparing to put in a blast when Marshall as
usual went to see Wimmer and the Indians who were at
work towards the lower end of the race. Then he sent a
young Indian for Brown to send him a plate. At his time
Brown and one of the Indians were whipsawing in the mill
yard. Brown was the top sawyer. He jumped from the
saw pit, remarking at the same time that he wondered what

1. Here is the only case I have discovered where Bigler makes a
definite mistake or tells an untruth: According to the fragment of the
original diary in the Pioneer Society his journal says "this day," not
"this afternoon."

Marshall wanted with a tin plate and went to the shanty and gave the Indian a plate. Just before we quit work, he [Marshall] came up and said he believed he had found a gold mine.[2] Some said there was no such good luck, but very little anyway was said at that time about it. He did not show us anything. Neither did he say he had any, but went off up to his own house on the side of the mountain. But before we went to bed, he came in and commenced talking with us, saying he believed he had found gold near the lower end of the race and, if I remember right, he told us that he tried to melt some and could not do it,[3] and he

2. The historic event of the discovery of the first gold flake is recorded in the original pocket diary in these words: "This day some kind of mettle was found in the tail of the race that looks like goald." This is the only direct source that fixes the day of the discovery. This entry and those of the preceding and following days, preserved in the original in the library of the Society of California Pioneers, are not in their pristine state, but are interpolated with additions in Bigler's own handwriting. Since Bigler usually wrote his entries on Sundays he had first written Sun., then obliterated it and corrected it to Monday. Most modern historians follow Marshall and Wimmer in the statement that the first particles of gold were found in the morning. But practically every other date given by Marshall or Wimmer is wrong. More justified would be a questioning of the wording of the brief entry above. It may be interpreted as an indication that Bigler had *seen* the "mettle" although the diary states that Marshall did not show the men any gold when he visited them before they went to bed. It would not be impossible that Marshall had seen the gold on Sunday afternoon, as sometimes claimed, but had not picked up the first flakes until Monday morning. Bigler might have erred when he wrote the story for Bancroft. But according to all indications, both days—when Marshall announced the finding and when he produced the first particles—were working days, and I have not been able to find a single instance where Bigler has fabricated such a convincing and logical story out of the whole cloth. Until proof to the contrary is established I believe I am justified in believing that Marshall discovered the first flakes in the afternoon of Monday, January 24 and told his men about it, and that it was Tuesday morning when he brought the first pieces in the crown of his hat to the mill yard.

3. This might be the reason that Marshall sent for a tin plate. Another possibility is, of course, that he might have wanted to separate the flakes from the dirt of the tailrace. That is quite natural although he did not know then that "panning" was the common primitive method of placer mining.

spoke to Brown and me saying, "Brown I want you and Bigler to shut down the head gate early in the morning; throw in a little sawdust, rotten leaves, and dirt and make all tight and I'll see what there is in the morning."

Accordingly the next morning we did as he told us while Marshall went alone down in the race, and we went in for our breakfast, and after we had breakfasted and come out, Brown to his sawing, Stephens to hewing, I to my drilling, every man at his own job, Marshall came up carrying his old white hat in his arm looking wonderfully pleased and good natured. There was a heavy smile on his countenance. Some of the boys said they knew in a minute as soon as they saw him that something was the matter. As he came up he said, "Boys, by G—d I believe I have found a gold mine" and set his hat on the work bench that stood in the mill yard. Every man gathered instantly around to see what he had and there, sure enough, on the top of the hat crown (knocked in a little) lay the pure stuff; how much I do not know, perhaps half an ounce, maybe more, from the smallest particle up to the size of a kernel of wheat or larger. The most of it was in very thin small flakes. The coarse were more round and in little cubes. In fact in most all shapes.[4] Every man fully expressed his

4. Now in the possession of the Bancroft Library is the so-called Wimmer nugget, which is claimed to have been the first piece of gold picked up that fateful day. There is, of course, no way of confirming or denying this. It is certain that Marshall gave the "nugget" to Wimmer, whose wife tested it by boiling it in strong lye. But Marshall claimed later that Mrs. Wimmer had spent it in a purchase, while Wimmer maintained that his wife preserved it.

I have discovered no evidence that the flake exhibited in the Smithsonian Institution has anything to do with "the first piece of gold ever discovered in the northern part of Upper California," Philip Bekeart's valiant efforts notwithstanding. Illustrations of the flake and Joseph L. Folsom's letter making the claim, in Egenhoff, pp. 48 ff., Bekeart, pp. 17 ff., and elsewhere. Since the identity of the first piece of gold is of interest mainly to collectors but not to historians we might as well resign ourselves with Bancroft: "The destiny of this first piece is lost to history."

conviction believing firmly it was gold although none of us had ever seen gold before in its native state. Azariah Smith pulled out a five-dollar piece (part of his soldier money) and we compared the dust with it. There seemed to be no difference as to color or weight, only that the coin looked a little brighter and rather more white. This we accounted for because of the alloy in it. Marshall turned about, and we all followed him, and in looking close, we could find particles here and there on the base rock and in seams and crevices. Conjectures were it must be rich, and from that time the fever set in and gold was on the brain. We, however, only spent a short time when every man went to work at his regular day labor; but gold was the talk.

In two or three days afterwards,[5] Marshall said he would take what gold we had found and go down to the Fort and have it tested, saying to us at the same time to keep it to ourselves until we knew what it was, etc. He was gone four days and when he returned and was asked what it was, his reply was, "Oh boys, by g——d, it is the pure stuff." Then he went on to tell what he had done. "I and the 'old cap,' " for that was the way he called Captain Sutter, "went in to a room and locked ourselves up and we were half a day trying it, and the regulars there wondered what the devil was up that Sutter and I should be locked up, and got an idea that perhaps I had found a quicksilver mine up here, for you know there was one down towards Monterey, found by a woman. We compared it with the encyclopedia and it agreed with it. We applied aqua fortis but it had nothing to do with it. We then weighed it in water. We took a basin with some water in it, then got our scales and put silver coin in one end and balanced the other with the dust in the air, then let it down gradually until the bal-

---

5. Three days afterwards, on the twenty-seventh (*New Helvetia Diary*).

ances came in contact with the water, and by g——d the gold went down and the silver up (motioned it out with his hands) and that told the story what it was.[6] "Sutter will be up in a day or two," he continued, "to examine and see for himself, and how we are getting on, etc."

About the third or fourth day afterwards at night Marshall entered our cabin and said: "Boys, the 'old cap' has come.[7] He is up at the house," and after talking a while and just before leaving he said, "Boys, the 'old cap' always carries his bottle with him, and I motion that we all throw in and give Henry some gold, and in the morning when you shut down the head gate let him take it down and sprinkle it all on the base rock, and when the old gentleman comes down and sees it, it will so excite him that he will bring out his bottle and treat." This was agreed to with a hearty laugh following the donation of dust from each one, for all had more or less gold.

So early the next morning, before Sutter came down, the water was shut off, and I went down into the tail race and sprinkled gold pretty plentifully, as Marshall had proposed. Just as we were completing our breakfast, we saw Marshall, Wimmer, and Sutter coming, walking side by side, while the old gentleman was in the middle, very well dressed, walking with a cane. At this we stepped out into the mill yard and met them, and after passing the common salutations, we were invited to go along and have a general time together in looking for gold. Right at this juncture one of Wimmer's little boys came running past us down into the race and picked up nearly every particle and came running back almost out of breath, meeting us, holding out his hand and saying, "Father, see what I have found." Sutter, as soon as he saw it, jabbed his cane into

---

6. Sutter himself tells the scene even more dramatically in his reminis-cences (Gudde, *Sutter,* pp. 190 ff.).
7. February 2 (*New Helvetia Diary*).

the ground saying, "By Jo, it is rich." Here the joke was against us. We dared not say a word, but let the boy claim and keep the gold, lest we lose our expected drink. The boy must have had somewhere between ten and twenty dollars. However, we all went down together and had a real time of prospecting. The boy had not completely cleaned the crevices and seams, so the Captain had the pleasure of finding and picking up here and there a few particles that had been left or overlooked by the boy.

The next move was that all the Indians who owned the land were called in forthwith, and Marshall and Sutter leased a large scope of the surrounding country, some ten or twelve miles square for three years, paying them down some clothing, such as shirts, pants, hats, handkerchiefs, a little flour, peas etc., with the promise to pay them so much every year till the lease ran out. Now it strikes me that Sutter was Indian agent, at least I know the tame Indians called him "Alcalde granda," [8] and any bargain they made with him they considered valid. After this agreement with the Indians they (Marshall and Sutter) sent Charles Bennett,[9] one of the mill hands, to Monterey to see Governor Mason and try and have the land secured to them as mill privileges, pasturage, and mineral privileges, as it bore strong indications of silver and lead (nothing said about gold). The Governor informed Mr. Bennett that as affairs were yet in rather an unsettled state between Uncle Sam and the Mexican government, he could do nothing for them.[10] The mill hands, however, respected their claims, knowing they at least were in possession of

8. In April, 1847, Sutter had been appointed Indian subagent for the district.

9. Bennett left the Fort for Monterey on February 8 (*New Helvetia Diary*).

10. The treaty of Guadalupe Hidalgo had been signed February 2, but the news had not yet reached Monterey. It was not officially proclaimed until July 4, after ratification by the two nations.

settlers' rights and had commenced improvements months before the gold was discovered.

Things continued to go on nicely, no one paying any attention to the gold except on Sundays; notwithstanding, there were many speculations among the men about how rich or how extensive it might be. Some and even the most of the hands had a strong desire and came very near letting the mill go and turn their attention to gold hunting, but still they were afraid lest they would lose in the long run more than they might make. They knew they were getting pretty fair wages for their labor on the mill and it was sure pay, while on the other hand there was a risk to run. That was the way we reasoned among ourselves, but when Sunday came, down into the tail race we would go. No other place seemed to strike us so favorable, and there we would pick and crevice with our jack and butcher knives, and we hardly ever failed to get three to eight dollars each and sometimes more. Still we were fearful to venture, and besides the mill being so near completed, we finally concluded to stick to the mill until she started.

These clear and concise statements must be considered the only true and authentic chronicle of the events until Bigler's unreliability is proved. The dean of California historians, Hubert Howe Bancroft, accepted Bigler's story as authentic and based on it his narratives of the discovery of gold. The second chapter of Volume VI of Bancroft's *History of California* and the fourth chapter of his *California Inter Pocula*, both published in 1888, after three-fourths of a century could still be considered as definitive and unsurpassed, except for one flaw: Bancroft treats the fabrication of an English writer, J. Tyrwhitt Brooks

[Henry Vizetelley], *Four Months among the Gold-finders,* as another important and authentic source.

Unfortunately, modern writers on the subject have confused the issue by taking seriously the unreliable reminiscences of another Mormon, James S. Brown.[11] He was also present on the day of discovery and he contradicts Bigler's statements in several instances by implication and in at least one place directly. According to Brown, the gold was discovered in the morning (not afternoon) of the twenty-fourth, and the incidents which Bigler connects with the discovery by Marshall took place on the preceding afternoon, January 23. To his statements modern historians have attached the same value as to Bigler.[12]

The oldest statement by Brown concerning the discovery of gold was made to L. H. Nichols, one of Bancroft's assistants, some time in November or December 1886.[13] This statement was disregarded by Bancroft in his *History of California* and in *California Inter Pocula.* Bancroft probably preferred to disregard Brown's account because it contradicted Bigler, whose journal Bancroft valued

---

11. Both Brown and Bigler were active members of the Church of the Latter-day Saints. They were Elders and repeatedly entrusted with missions to foreign lands. Both loved to tell their life stories. But here the similarity ends. Bigler lived in very moderate circumstances all his life and had only one average family. Brown was apparently well-to-do, for he had four wives and thirty-one children, and in 1952 his posterity amounted to eight hundred and sixty individuals. With Bigler the truth came first and the Church second. With Brown it was reversed: his writings are dictated by the desire to place the Church and his own person on a higher level than they deserve. He lacks Bigler's modesty and objectivity.

12. James Peter Zollinger in his standard biography of Sutter; Aubrey Neasham in his thorough account, "Sutter's Sawmill" in the California Historical Society *Quarterly* of 1947; John W. Caughey, the author of the excellent, *Gold Is the Cornerstone;* Owen C. Coy, in his *Gold Days.* If it had not been for the fact that historians take Brown seriously I should not even have listed Brown's writings, just as I disregard the yarn that Allen and Avery spin in *California Gold Book* for the benefit of Jennie Wimmer.

13. Manuscript in Bancroft Library.

highly, but it is also possible that Bancroft's manuscript for the volume was already too far advanced to include Brown's remarks.

The important point in Brown's account is that he claims he was with Marshall on the afternoon of January 23, and that Marshall had sent him to the cabin for a pan and had tried to wash gold out of the decomposed granite on the bottom of the tail race, but had found nothing. The next morning Marshall had come to the mill yard with the first fragments of gold. Brown says he was whip-sawing, not with an Indian but with James Barger, and not as the top sawyer, but in the pit. When Brown saw what Marshall had in his hat Brown "picked up a piece and put it in my mouth and twisted it and then exclaimed so boys could hear me: gold! gold!"

However, January 23, when Brown alleges he helped "pan" for gold, was a Sunday.[14] Brown's account as well as all other sources leave no doubt that both days in question were working days. In addition to being a Sunday, on which work was done only in an emergency, and none by the Mormons, the twenty-third was the day on which the Mormons Bigler, Brown, Barger, Johnson, and Smith moved into their cabin which they had built after their altercation with Jennie Wimmer. The entry in Bigler's diary of Sunday, January 23, as given in the fragment of the original pocket diary, runs: "Clear. This day Myself

---

14. It is significant that Smith, who regularly wrote his journal on Sunday, has no entry for the twenty-third. Was he too busy moving and fixing up the new house with the others and did not have time to make his customary Sunday entry in his diary? The next Sunday, the thirtieth, he entered: "Mr. Marshall having arrived [after the 16th!] we got liberty of him, and built a small house down by the mill; and last Sunday we moved into it in order to get rid of the brawling, partial mistress and cook for ourselves. This week Mr. Marshall found some pieces of (as we all suppose) Gold, and he has gone to the Fort for the purpose of finding out. It is found in the raceway in small pieces; some have been found that would weigh five dollars [!]"

and four others moved into a house that we had built last week." This evidence alone may not be sufficient to show conclusively that Bigler was right and Brown was wrong. But on January 24, 1894, Brown wrote on the occasion of the forty-sixth anniversary of the discovery of gold, an account which was published under the impressive title *California Gold: An Authentic History of the First Find* by the Pacific Press Publishing Company in Oakland, California. In this account Brown gives Sutter and Marshall some credit for the discovery. But if it had not been for the Mormons, "the State of California would have waited indefinitely to have been developed and to be christened the 'Golden State,' and that entrance to San Francisco Bay might never have received the title of the 'Golden Gate.' " The latter statement might be excused, for even today some people believe that the Golden Gate received its name from the discovery of gold although it was named by Frémont in 1846 for entirely different reasons. But his statement that the Mormons were responsible for the discovery of gold, because Sutter did not decide to build the mill in Coloma until the Mormons arrived and provided the workmen, contradicts the facts.[15]

Another statement which can easily be contradicted is Brown's claim that he was in charge of the Indian laborers at the mill because he had "picked up sufficient of the Indian dialect to direct the Indians." Brown claims in other places that he was an accomplished linguist. That may be true, but he was hardly so gifted that he could pick up the Southern Maidu dialect almost at first hearing. Above all, the sources agree with Bigler that the man in charge

---

15. It is true that the Mormons arrived just at the right time, and their arrival may even have accelerated Sutter's project to start building the sawmill at the end of August. But the grist mill as well as the sawmill were planned years before, and building had been postponed because of the Mexican War.

of the Indian workmen was Peter Wimmer, who had been in the country for some time and had been at the mill site in Coloma before Brown and the Mormons arrived.

Least credible is Brown's claim that he submitted his story "to be filed away as a true history," and that five fellow Mormons witnessed Brown's account as "a true and correct statement of the first discovery of gold in California." Four of these five gentlemen who knew this "true" history are listed on the roster of the Mormon Battalion and all five were employed by Sutter—but none were present at Sutter's mill when gold was discovered. Israel Evans, to be sure, came to Coloma on September 29, 1847, together with Bigler, but he was working at the grist mill in Natoma at the time of the discovery.[16]

Brown's account was reprinted in a curious booklet dedicated "To the Posterity of James S. Brown" and entitled *A Compilation of Authentic Information Regarding the First Discovery of Gold in California January 24, 1848*. It was published in 1953 by some of the eight hundred and sixty proud descendants who are true to the carelessness of their progenitor in treating historical facts. The "true story" which was published in 1894, the year of the mid-winter fair, is stated to have been written in 1897 when Brown and the three other survivors were guests at the Golden Jubilee and Mr. Brown remained behind in San Francisco to write his "authentic history." The five witnesses certified to the "true story" but did not claim to have been present at the discovery, and even Brown does not say that the witnesses were at Coloma but

16. At the time of writing his "true" story there were three men still living in Utah who had been present at the mill on January 24, 1848. In fact, in an appendix to his pamphlet Brown prints a letter by Bigler (misspelled Beglar), dated "St. George, Utah, Dec. 20th, 1885." Brown must have had good reasons not to ask these three gentlemen to certify his story.

"at the place," which can be interpreted as somewhere on
Sutter's property (*Life of a Pioneer*, p. 106). But the
compilers of the booklet boldly state: "This story is at-
tested by five other members of the Battalion who were at
Sutter's mill at the time of the first discovery." [17]

To the historian is thus presented this problem: both
accounts, as far as the sequence of events is concerned,
are logically possible; but all of Brown's and some of
Bigler's statements were made years later, and there is no
corroborating evidence for either narration of the exact
time and the detailed circumstances of the event. The other
eyewitnesses of the twenty-fourth of January, 1848, who
wrote about it, James Marshall, Azariah Smith, Peter and
Jennie Wimmer, either do not touch upon the day before
the discovery or their accounts can be easily refuted.
Hence one has to decide for Bigler or for Brown. An objective historian will have to decide definitely for Henry
W. Bigler, whose style is logical and convincing and who
has not been caught with any deliberate misstatements or
unproved claims.

VIII.
THE FIRST
PROSPECTOR: 1848

The first that I have any knowledge of gold being found in
any other place aside from the race was on Sunday the

17. The same curious compilation also contains a reprint of the story
of gold discovery as given to a reporter of the San Francisco *Examiner*,
during the great San Francisco mid-winter Fair of 1894. The absurdities
in it are so glaring that the interview does not deserve consideration.

SUTTER'S MILL

FROM FRANK SOULÉ, *Annals of San Francisco* (1855)

HUMBOLDT RIVER   BY F. W. EGGLOFSTEIN, IN *Pacific Railroad Reports*, VOL. II (1855)

PHOTOGRAPH BY COURTESY OF BANCROFT LIBRARY

sixth of February. That morning I said I was going over
the river opposite the mill to see if I could find any, point-
ing to some bare rock directly opposite the saw mill. Mr.
Barger said he would go with me, and over we went taking nothing but our jackknives.[1] Indeed we knew nothing
about washing it out. I believe the whole pile of mill hands
were perfectly green. There were no such things thought
of by us as long toms, or short toms, or rockers, or sluices.
I believe there was something said about tin pans, but we
had none. Our only way was to pick it up grain by grain
as we found it lying on the bare rocks, or feeling after it
in the seams and crevices of the exposed rocks with our
knives. But, as I was going to say, we went over while the
rest stuck to the tailrace. At night, Barger and myself between us had about ten dollars according to the way we
calculated, which was like this: We had already made a
pair of light wooden scales and we had a little silver coin.
We put, for instance, a twelve-and-one-half-cent piece in
one end and balanced the other end with our dust. This
we reckoned at two dollars. If we had enough to pull down
a quarter of a dollar, that we counted four dollars, and
so on.

I seemed to be the only one in the crowd that had gold
badly on the brain, and it was one Saturday, the twelfth
of February in the afternoon, when I threw my pick out
of my hands (for I had been at work with some others cutting down the race) and asked Brown to lend me his gun,
and I would go down the river and try and kill some ducks.
He told me to do so, but it was not ducks I was after. I
took the gun and put out down the river. As soon as I was
fairly out of sight I commenced eying every likely looking
spot where I thought there might be gold. When I got

1. When Sutter visited the mill on February 2, he good-naturedly had
not only brought a bottle from New Helvetia's distillery, but a number
of pocket knives for the men to make their gold-hunting easier.

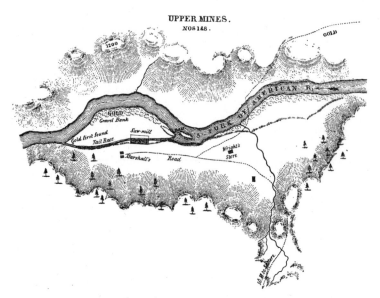

about half a mile below the mill, I discovered on the op-posite side a place that looked like there had been a slide some day and the rocks were naked of earth. The river was pretty deep and rapid. I ventured across by taking off every rag I had on. When I got to the place I could see several particles exposed to view lying in the seams of the rocks.[2]

The next day was Sunday and it rained most all day. I, however, said nothing but went back and picked up eight dollars or half an ounce.

I worked that week on the mill and about it till next Sunday, the twentieth, when I returned saying nothing to anyone and picked up a little over an ounce.[3] Monday, the twenty-first of February, I sowed and harrowed in three acres of peas for Marshall, and it was about this time

2. In the Hittell version he states that he took the afternoon off be-cause he was tired and did not feel good.

3. Utah version: "Went to my gold mine and picked up about seven-teen dollars worth." An ounce was worth sixteen to seventeen dollars.

THE FIRST PROSPECTOR: 1848

I wrote to Jesse Martin, Israel Evans, and Ephraim Green (three mess mates of mine while in the Battalion) who were at work on Sutter's flouring mill, and informed them that we had found gold at the sawmill, but to keep it to themselves unless it would be to someone who could keep a secret. Mr. Marshall did not want it known until further development, not knowing how extensive it was.[4]

February 22. When we arose that morning we found the ground white with snow that fell during the night. The upper frame of the sawmill, or top story if you please, was to have been raised that day. Marshall came in about the time we were at breakfast and said, "Boys it is going to be pretty slippery today and rather bad about putting up the frame. You may work if you see fit, or let it alone."

Elic [Alexander] Stephens said he believed he would not work but go to mending and patching his old britches. Brown said he did not care about working as it was going to be rather disagreeable and dangerous. He would go to work and cook a mess of peas, as we had not had any for some time. In this way all found an excuse to lay over for the day, and as I was about the only hunter in the pile, I spoke up and said, "Brown, if you will lend me your gun, I will go ahunting." "There is the gun, take it," was the reply.

---

4. By this time it was already too late to try to keep the discovery a secret. On February 11, a teamster, Jacob Wittmer, had delivered provisions to the sawmill and let out the news at the Fort when he wanted to celebrate by buying a bottle of liquor in Smith's store and pay for it in gold (*New Helvetia Diary*). When Charles Bennett left the Fort for Monterey on February 8 with Sutter's application for a preëmption of the Coloma district, "he left in his wake groups of people talking about Sutter's gold mine" (Gudde, *Sutter* pp. 197–205). However Bigler's indiscretion led to the discovery of the rich diggings on Mormon Island and indirectly to Sam Brannan's initiation of the gold rush. Scott, *Brannan* (pp. 215 ff.), retells Bigler's account of the discovery as if he had told it to Brannan directly in Smith's store at the Fort over a bottle of brandy.

I struck out up the mountain to look for deer, but when I gained the summit a little west of south of the mill, I changed my notion and also my course, turned directly to the right and made for the river. I did not care any more for deer than I did for ducks. It was the same old place I wanted to visit where I had been just the Sunday or two previous. As usual I stripped and waded over. I could hardly keep my feet. The water came up pretty high on me and swift as a mill tail and cold. When I got across, I concluded to strike fire and warm up, but I could not do it. My hands and fingers were so benumbed with the cold that I could not hold the flint and steel. I then undertook to catch fire from the gun, she being a caplock, but some way or other in crossing the river the load got wet and with all my ingenuity I could not set her off. I was obliged to do all my own dancing alone; and what was more aggravating, while I was cutting up all kinds of capers over the rocks I could see the yellow pieces lying as if they were looking at me saying, pick me up if you can. Now notwithstanding snow had fallen and the ground white that morning, yet it was so light that on the sand bars and bare rocks it had melted. The day was cloudy and yet warm so at times there were heavy mists of rain. I, however, soon warmed up myself and went to work. I felt close in every crevice, and finally down near the waters edge, in the sand, I began to find it. Here I sat all the balance of the day in one position, all hunched up, picking it out grain by grain, from the smallest particle up to a single nugget worth over five dollars. And laying it on the top of my cap with the point of my knife—when the first thing I knew, I could not see. It was dark and being so excited and without thinking, that when I arose to straighten myself, I yelled with pain. A person could have heard me quite a distance. I thought my back was broken. After a few grunts and groans I made my way up the river, and when I came to the mill dam, I called for Brown to bring the raft (three or four pine logs pinned together) and set me over.

The boys some way or other had smelled a rat and wanted to know why I did not cross in the morning and why it was I was so late and what luck I had, etc. I pulled the rag out of my pocket. No, not that exactly either. (I will tell the truth, Mr. Bancroft.) I had tied it up for safe keeping in the corner of my shirt tail. The boys weighed it for me and said I had a little short of one ounce and a half of clean gold dust.[5]

On the following Sunday, which was the twenty-seventh, five of us went to that same spot and spent the day hunting in the sand, frequently laying on our bellies, scratching and hunting for it.[6] The day was warm and pleasant and it was at this date at night when three men from below (Mormon boys), namely Sidney Willis, Wilford Hudson, and a Mr. [Levi] Fifield, came with their guns and blankets on their backs. They had learned through the letter I had written, about the twentieth, to Martin, Green, and Evans that we had discovered gold in the race. It was told to them as a secret, and they let on to the mill hands below that they were going up to the sawmill on a visit to see the boys and spend a few days hunting deer. It was dusk when they arrived. Mr. Marshall happened to be in our house when they came, and as gold was all the talk, Marshall sat until a late hour before he left for his lodging and in a first-rate good humor as he most always was.

---

5. This memorable Tuesday of the 116th anniversary of Washington's birthday may be marked down as the beginning of the gold rush on a limited scale, that is, before Brannan imparted the news to the world. "All hands came very near leaving off work to turn our attention to hunting gold" (Utah version).

6. According to the Utah version, they picked up thirty-three dollars' worth although the place that Bigler had discovered on the twenty-second was under water.

Hudson asked him the privilege of prospecting the next morning in the tailrace, which was readily granted, and the next morning, while breakfast was preparing, the three boys went into the race, and it was not long before Hudson picked out of the bank of the race with his butcher knife a nugget that according to our way of testing was worth a little short of six dollars.

They remained with us until Thursday morning, the second of March, when Willis and Hudson concluded to return back to the flouring mill by following the river and prospect all the way down it. Fifield said he would not go that way but take the road. I accompanied Fifield back, and when all four of us met at the flouring mill (at where Brighton now stands) the two boys reported that they had found a few particles at one place only. I saw the particles and passed my judgment that there was not to exceed fifty cents worth in very fine particles, so trifling a prospect in their estimation, that they had no notion of examining it any further.[7] But Ephraim Green and Ira Willis, a brother to Sidney, kept coaxing and urging them to go back, and they would go with them and examine close; it might be rich, said they. But it was several days before they got them persuaded to do so.

I, however, returned to the sawmill and went to work as usual, when on Saturday the eleventh of March, Mr. Marshall started the sawmill. It was a curiosity to the Indians, and the very Indian who said it was a lie, that no such outfit could be made, was completely beat. He lay on his belly where he could have a fair view from the bank, but near the saw, and lay there for two hours watching it. He was taken with it and said it was "wano" [8] and wanted to be a sawyer right off. That is, he wished to help saw.

7. They did not realize that they had discovered the place which soon became the earliest of the really rich diggings, Mormon Island.
8. *Bueno.*

The next day was Sunday. The saw ran all day and cut
very well, and for aught I know, it was the first sawmill
built in California. There was not quite fall enough yet
in the tailrace, and the week was mostly spent in completing the race, and Sunday the nineteenth, was spent as
usual in hunting gold. I disremember what the whole pile
of us got. My journal says I picked up about two ounces.[9]

This week I took charge of the Indians learning them
how to chop, cutting down saw log timber. They seemed
to be quite willing and anxious to learn, but very awkward.
Every now and then they would slap the axe into their legs
or foot. I oft times felt sorry for them. Marshall and Sutter seemed to treat them well and to pay them well, let
them have clothing, meat and peas, knives, etc.[10]

I continued working this way until Friday, the seventh
of April, when Stephens, Brown, and myself set out on
horseback for the Fort to have a settlement with Captain
Sutter. We got a late start, made only a few miles and
camped in the mountains. The next evening we arrived at
the lower camp or flouring mill. We found the mill not
near completed. The frame was up, and whether it ever
was started I never learned.[11] Here we learned that Willis
and Hudson with several of the boys were up the river
getting gold and had been for several days, but how they

---

9. "I was the luckiest one and picked up 31 dollars" (Hittell and
Utah).

10. The entries during the weeks following the starting of the mill
are more complete in the other versions. Under March 26, both other
printed versions report that all hands hunted for gold and that Bigler
found six dollars' worth. Under date of April 2, Bigler records in
Hittell that he found a new place for gold and got thirty dollars. In
the Utah version Bigler also summarizes the experiences since January
24, without adding anything essential that was not recorded in the Bancroft version under the proper date.

11. The grist mill was never started. The often praised loyalty of the
Mormons did not work here. Mormons and non-Mormons left the mill
for the gold fields.

were making it, no one seemed to know. I discovered, however, there was a fearfulness among the hands about leaving their work and go on uncertainty. Notwithstanding, some of the party had been down and reported they thought the digging was going to be good. I suppose in truth they were like Marshall was; they did not care about letting all the world know about it until they knew that there was a chance for all.

The next day, Sunday, April 9,[12] pretty much all the boys came together to talk over matters and things in regard to making arrangements for going up to the Great Salt Lake and come to some understanding when we should make the start etc. The decision was that all be ready by the first of June, except eight who were ready and expected to start with an express the next Saturday, though I believe to the States. It was further decided that we send out a few men as pioneers before that time to pioneer out a route across the Sierra Nevada and if possible find a much nearer way than to go the Truckee route and thus shun crossing the very deep and rapid Truckee River twenty-seven times. We were informed by Mr. Brannan we would have to do so if we went that route. The meeting also decided that Captain Sutter be informed of our intentions and time of starting for home, so as to give him time to arrange his business accordingly. It was also motioned and carried that Mr. Browett be the man to inform him of our intended move, and also of what we wished as to the number of cattle, and horses, and oxen, cows, brood mares and mules, etc. We would also take two small brass

---

12. Beginning with April 9, 1848, the Utah version was literally copied from the Bancroft version (*Utah Historical Quarterly*, V, 148 ff.). The Utah version kept the original spelling and corrected only the punctuation. The introductory note to this section states that it is a "true copy of the original journal," which is to be understood that it is a true copy of the Bancroft version.

pieces (cannons) which we understood he offers for sale. We wished to get seeds of various kinds, as well as vines.

April 10. Stephens, Brown, and myself called on the Captain. We found him very busy, and learning his books were not posted, a settlement with him was omitted for the present.

April 11. We mounted our horses and set out at rather a late hour for the sawmill, where we intended to turn our attention wholly to gold hunting for a short time. This was our calculation when we left to return, having an understanding with Mr. Marshall to dig on shares, he furnishing all the grub and tools, so long as we worked on his claims or land. We encamped that night about fifteen miles from the flouring mill on a creek.

April 12. This morning, while our horses were filling up on the grass, we concluded to prospect a little in the creek and we soon found it and spent half the day having nothing but our knives and the two small basins we had with us to sip our coffee out of. We got about ten dollars. For supper and breakfast we baked our bread on flat stones. We straddled our horses and struck out to hunt the boys, who were not far from this place digging gold. We struck in close to the river, and following up its banks we soon found them.

We found seven of the boys at work. They had taken out that day two hundred and fifty dollars. This was the spot where the few particles were found by the Messrs. Willis and Hudson on the second of March while returning from the sawmill and thought it not much account, and this is the place that afterwards went by the name of "Mormon Island." Here for the first time I saw an improvement for washing out gold. That was with Indian baskets. They had one or two old baskets and they would wash out from twenty-five cents to two dollars at a basket full of dirt. I suppose they were about the size of [an] eight- or ten-quart basin—tin pans in those days were scarce. The names of the men who were here at work were Sidney Willis, Ira Willis, Willford Hudson, Jesse B. Martin, and Ephraim Green. The other two I disremember, but I think they were Israel Evans and James Sly. It was about this time that one or both of the Willises had business that called them from their mining to the Fort, and it strikes me they went to Yerba Buena; at all events they met with Sam Brannan and let him in to the secret. Mr. Brannan told them he could secure the mine as church property and advised for all the Battalion boys to go to work in the mine and pay one-tenth to him and he would turn it over to the church as their tithing, with the understanding, at the same time, that he was to come in with the Willises and Hudson having a share with them in their claim. This they did.[13] Mr. Brannan at that time was publishing a paper at Yerba Buena called the *California Star*. He then published forthwith in his paper that gold was found by the Mormon boys in rich abundance on the South Fork of the American River, and hence it went that the first discovery of gold was made by the "Mormons." I suppose there are thousands to this day who believe they were the first who found the gold in California in 1848.[14] In this way all California and, I may say, all the world was on the move in a very short time for the land of gold. I will now return.

April 13. We arrived at the Coloma sawmill and the

13. At least until Governor Mason told them that Mr. Brannan had a perfect right to collect the money as long as they were fools enough to pay him.

14. This significant statement is faithfully copied in the Utah version but not in the Hittell and Ledger versions. Brannan doubtless spread the rumor, but not through his paper.

next day commenced and continued to work in the mines until about the middle of June, when we left Coloma to prepare and start for our homes in the valley of the mountains.[15] While working in the mines we must have worked under great disadvantages. I wanted badly to get an Indian basket, but some way or other failed, and if I remember right, we had but one tin pan and that was a small one. I used a wooden tray that we had to knead our dough in. Elic [Alexander] Stephens dug out a wooden dish that he used to wash in, and we carried our dirt in sacks on our backs from some small dry gulches for five or six hundred yards to the river and washed it out. These little gulches must have been exceedingly rich, as I can now fancy, for where we got one dollar then, they could later get hundreds. These diggings were about one mile below the sawmill on the north side of the river among some flats of land. In less than three weeks after our return to Coloma

---

15. From here until the start of the trek for Salt Lake Bigler summarized and amplified his journal for the Bancroft version. The entries in the Huntington version for April read as follows:

Friday 14th. This morning we put out for hunting the 'platter' [plata] as the Spaniards call it. I found $11.00.

Sat. 15th. I found 22 dollars worth.

Sunday 16th. I picked up seven dollars.

Tuesday 18th. I carried dirt on my back five or six hundred yards to the River and washed it and got eleven dollars. I used a wooden tray we use to knead dough in, to wash and gether my gold.

Wed. 19th. I washed out 18 dollars; Brown and Steven found about the same each, we find it in small gulches leading to the River but have no water, and carry the dirt to the River to wash out the "Platter."

Thursday 20th. Brown went to hunt our horses as they were seen following off a mair [mare] and colt he had lately bought; today I hunted for gold and got 18 dollars.

Friday 21st. I found thirty dollars and Stevens 25 dollars. Brown returned without finding the horses, saw no sign of them leaving the Range.

Sat. 22. Found 25 dollars, Stevens 45 dollars and Brown 9 $ 20 cts.

Sunday 23rd. Like Christians we kept the Sabbath day while a lot of Gentiles came into our camp to look for gold but found none.

the Californians began to come in thick and fast, having learned of the discovery through the *California Star*, and our little gulches were soon lined from end to end by gold diggers, who already began to dispute Marshall's claims to the land and commenced mining wherever they pleased. Among the number that came in was an old Sonorian. He used a cotton sheet. He spread it down near a hole of water (a little slanting) put his pay dirt on it, then straddled the hole, and with his shovel he would throw water on to it, and thus wash away the dirt leaving the gold sticking to the cloth. Brown and myself saw that that was quite an improvement by the side of our wooden dishes, and we adopted that plan for a while.

The snow seemed to lie on the mountains a little longer than we expected; and the mines also became more attractive, so that our pioneers did not go out so soon to hunt a pass across the mountains as at first expected. But when the time came and while leaving Coloma on our way down to Sutter's Fort, there to make preparations for our intended move, we met several parties making their way into the mines, and it seemed to me that all California was on the hunt of gold. I saw a schoolteacher, I think his name was a Mr. Maston,[16] who said he had a school of forty pupils in San Francisco (perhaps the first school ever started there). He said the excitement was so great that everybody had left, and there were no children to come to school; so he thought he would leave, too, and go and seek his fortune with the rest. A Mr. Benjamin Hawkins [17] told me only a few days ago that he was in San Francisco at the time Samuel Brannan made the announcement of the dis-

---

16. J. D. Marston had opened a private school, the first in San Francisco, April, 1847.

17. A former member of the Mormon Battalion.

covery of gold. He said Brannan took his hat off and swung it, shouting aloud in the streets that gold was found, etc. The inhabitants of the place seemed to be panic-struck and so excited and in such a hurry to be off, that some of the mechanics left their work, not taking time even to take off their aprons, and he himself (Hawkins) struck out and bought up all the Indian baskets he could (fifteen). Some of the boys laughed at him for it, but he found them to be no drug as he sold them afterwards for fifteen dollars each. A large crowd went ahead of him. When he and those who were with him, arrived at the American fork a few miles below Mormon Island, they found a boat lying among some driftwood. They took it out and lashed it on a couple of horses and packed it a short distance up the river and crossed over the north side, where they found a place that suited them. There they commenced work unobserved by anyone, for everybody was still farther up the river. At this time he said rockers began to be made, and one had been made above somewhere and had escaped and floated down the river, and they saved it and in one day washed out between three and four thousand dollars. He told me there were five of them, namely himself, old man Haskel,[18] and Fayette Shepherd. The other two, I disremember their names.

18. A George Haskell was also a member of the Battalion. But "old man Haskel" probably was Ashbel Hascall, who had come to California on the *Brooklyn* (*Utah Historical Quarterly* XXV, p. 257.

IX.

ACROSS THE SIERRA AND
ALONG THE HUMBOLDT: 1848

June 17. This morning myself and two others set out on horseback from where Brighton now stands,[1] taking our blankets, a little grub, and our axes to go into the mountains, or rather into the foothills, to find a suitable place to rally, from which point all who were intending to go up to the Great Salt Lake would start.

The next day, the eighteenth, we found a spot we thought would do—a distance, as we thought, about forty-five miles from the flouring mill, the place we left the day before, and I should conclude from what I have heard, that this place was not far from Placerville. We gave the name of our little valley, Pleasant Valley.[2] Here we felled pine timber and built a large corral. On the twenty-first some of the boys arrived with our band of loose horses, and the twenty-two wagons began to roll in, mostly drawn by oxen, followed by our cows and calves. The gathering continued until the second of July.[3] On the morning of the third a general move was made, except myself and a few others, who were detained in finding our oxen, when on the fourth, about 11:00 A.M., we rolled out after the camp, taking the divide between the American River and the Cosumnes.

1. The gristmill by Natoma.
2. Eight miles southeast of Placerville between Cosumnes River and Weber Creek. Still so called.
3. According to the Hittell version, they whiled away their time by washing gold with considerable success.

We made about ten miles, and just as we began to prepare for camping we heard the cannon from the front camp and were reminded that this was the birthday of American Independence.

July 5. Made an early start, still keeping the divide, and by 9:00 A.M. we rolled up to the front camp. Here they had concluded to stop a few days, as they had found a nice little valley (though about two miles to the south of the waters of the Cosumnes) for our stock and send out some men to examine the route and look for three of our company, viz. Browett, Allen, and Cox, who had left our camp on the twenty-fifth of June to look out for a pass while the company was gathering, and as yet we had not heard anything from them, and the camp began to feel uneasy about them. Accordingly, we sent out ten men to look for them, while the rest of us took the stock down into the little valley, which we called Sly's Park after one of our men who found it and there built a couple corrals, and we awaited the return of the ten men.[4]

They returned on the fourteenth of July and reported they had seen nothing of the three men, neither any signs. After passing a certain point they had discovered a pass but it would have to be worked.

July 15. This morning, myself and three others went ahead with axes to cut brush and roll rocks out of the way for our wagons and packs. My journal supposed a wagon never had been here before since these mountains were made and for aught I know, not even a white man. Our camp made about eight miles and encamped on the top of the divide about one mile from water.

July 16. Cutting our way as yesterday, the road very bad; broke a coupling pole to one of the wagons; made

---

4. Still so called. Named for James C. Sly, formerly a private in Company C of the Battalion, but a sort of a leader.

about eight miles and encamped on the waters of the Cosumnes. This we called Camp Creek.[5]

July 17. Today we had bad road and a great deal of brush to cut; broke an axle tree; made eight or ten miles and camped at Leek Spring, a fine spring with plenty of leeks and grass about it.

July 18. Camp laid by to hunt some stock that was lost out of the herd yesterday. While myself and four others went to work the road, which we did for about ten miles, and as we were returning to camp we found the place where we supposed our three pioneers had camped by a large spring, running from the mountains into the Cosumnes. Near where they had their fire, was the appearance of a fresh grave. Some of us thought it might be an Indian grave, as near it was an old wickey up, but the more we looked at it, the more we felt there lay the three men. When we got back to camp all the lost stock was found, and we made a report of the road and the grave, etc. That evening the camp was called together and organized more perfectly by appointing captains of tens and we also appointed Lieutenant Thompson Captain [6] over the whole camp, in case there should be any fighting to do. That night for the first time we put out camp guard. Our numbers were as follows, forty-five men and one woman (Sargent Wm. Coray's wife), two small brass pieces bought of Sutter, seventeen wagons, one hundred fifty horses and about the same of cattle, and I believe every man had a musket.

July 19. Rolled out from Leek Spring; had hard, heavy pulling, the road very rocky in places; broke our new

---

5. An affluent to the Cosumnes River. Still so called.

6. Samuel Thompson, former second lieutenant of Company C of the Battalion.

PREPARING THE EVENING MEAL FROM A SKETCH BY WILLIAM JOSEPH JACKSON

REPRODUCED WITH THE KIND PERMISSION OF CLARENCE S. JACKSON

WEBER RIVER NEAR SALT LAKE BY F. W. EGGLOFSTEIN, IN *Pacific Railroad Reports*, VOL. II (1855)

axle tree, and in passing over a snowbank Mr. J. Holmes' wagon broke down. Made only five or six miles and encamped at the spring near the fresh grave; determining to satisfy ourselves, it was soon opened. We were shocked at the sight. There lay the three murdered men robbed of every stitch of clothing, lying promiscuously in one hole about two feet deep. Two of them were lying on their faces. Allen was lying on his back and had the appearance that an ax had been sunk into his face and that he had been shot in the eye. The blood seemed fresh still oozing from their wounds. When we came to examine around about, we found arrows lying plentifully on the ground, many of them bloody and broken. Examining still closer, the rocks were stained with blood, and Mr. Allen's purse of gold dust was lying about a rod from the grave. The gold was still in the sack. It was known by several of the boys who had seen him make it. He had attached a buckskin string of sufficient length so as to put it over his head and around his neck and letting the purse hang in his bosom inside of his clothes. Some thought their guns and saddles might be in their grave with them, for they had set out leaving the camp having each a riding animal and a pack mule. At the time they left camp, they were advised not to go but wait until all the camp was ready for a start; but they seemed restless and anxious to be on the move towards home and so left, saying they would travel slowly and hunt out the best way across the Sierra Nevada and would meet us somewhere in the mountains.

July 20. Last night just before lying down and before the guard was posted, something or other gave our horses and cattle a dreadful affright, supposed to be either grizzlies or Indians. The thundering of the running stock fairly shook the ground and was like an earthquake. Lieutenant Thompson ordered to "limber up a cannon and let her speak once." The guard was soon put out, but nothing more occurred.

All was quiet till morning, when we found more than one-third of the stock missing. We lay here all day; sent men in all directions hunting up lost stock. In the afternoon we enclosed the grave with granite rocks to prevent wild beasts from tearing them out and to stand as a monument to all who may chance to pass that way. We judged they were killed the second night out, which would make it the twenty-seventh of June. We cut the following inscription on a balsam fir that stood near the grave: "To the memory of Daniel Browett, Ezrah H. Allen, and Henderson Cox, who were supposed to have been murdered and buried by Indians on the night of the twenty-seventh of June, A.D. 1848." We called this place Tragedy Spring.[7]

July 21. Having found all our stock, except one or two mules, we hooked on and moved about four miles and camped on what we called Rock Creek and built a corral by felling timber and piling up brush. The mountains well overlaid with large masses of rocks, in the little valleys plenty of leeks, young grass, and clover, with here and there a large bank of snow.

July 22. Camp laid by, while myself and fifteen others worked a road to the top of the mountain; some six miles from the top we saw several small lakes, some of which I was told abounded with trout.[8] I passed over snow more than two feet deep and saw banks ten and perhaps fifteen feet deep. This day I gathered flowers with one hand and

---

7. Still so called.

8. From here to September 26 the Bancroft version can be compared with the Day Book, to all appearances a copy of the only lengthy fragment of the original pocket diaries known to me. The Bancroft version is a little more detailed. The few dates that can be compared with the Hittell version, which ends with July 30, differ essentially.

snow with the other. There were plenty of chickens in the timber resembling the prairie chickens. At evening we returned to camp, tired and hungry, although we carried lunch with us.

July 23. In camp all day.

July 24. Moved about six miles and camped just over the summit.[9] Two wagons broke down and two were upset. Two Indians came in to stay all night.

July 25. Laid by while some went repairing wagons, others watching stock, while others again worked a road down the mountain some two miles.

July 26. Moved to the foot of the mountain and camped near a lake. This we call Lake Valley. As usual we broke down again; an axle tree snapped in two. This afternoon we sent out ten men to explore and hunt a pass across the mountain.

July 27. Made some road. Twenty Indians came into camp, all armed with bows and arrows, but laid them by while in camp. Late in the afternoon our ten men returned but had made no new discovery.

July 28. Moved three miles and made an early encampment at the head of the American Fork near or at the summit of the great Sierra Nevada. Here we soon built a corral sufficiently large to hold all our stock. Several Indians were seen, some peeking out from behind and over rocks; two however came into camp. Some of our party caught a young fawn. They marked the youngster and let him go. This afternoon we worked and made a road across the mountain.[10]

July 29. Moved across about one mile and half and camped at the head of what we called Hope Valley, as we

9. More explicitly in the Day Book: "Camped on the north side of the mountain."

10. In the Day Book the many lakes are mentioned under this date.

began to have hope.[11] In crossing over we broke one wagon.

July 30. Worked and made a road for about two miles and moved camp about eight miles and encamped on what we called Pass Creek at the head of a canyon. Here we expect to lay by for several days in order to work a road through the canyon about four miles and very bad.

July 31. A general turnout to work on the road, making fording places to cross the creek. Considerable digging to do and rolling rocks out of the way.

August 1. Clear and frosty this morning. Fifteen turned out and worked on the road. Some went a-fishing and caught a lot of trout. Here grows the first wild flax I ever saw. Some of it is in blow and some in the bowl.

August 2. Working as yesterday in the canyon, except myself who went a-fishing. Caught twelve nice trout.

August 3. Road working. In the afternoon fell a little rain and snow. We were overtaken today by thirteen of our boys with pack animals. They had left the mines five days ago. We finished our road.

August 4. Moved through the canyon, all safe. Four Indians came into camp.

August 5. At about seven o'clock we were on the march. Good road, made about twelve miles and camped on Carson River, though at that time we had no name for it; only the one we gave it, and that was Pilot River. One of our men killed a fine antelope. Several of the natives visited our camp. The mountains seem to be all on fire and the valley full of smoke.

August 6. Continued down Carson River passed a hot spring. Camped in the bend of the river. Here Mr. [Addison] Pratt killed a rattlesnake, which gave the name Rattlesnake Camp. At night we could see as if there were

11. Still so called.

118

a hundred fires in the California mountains. Made, no doubt, by Indians. Some think it is a signal to other Indians of distress. Others say it is for peace, and some say it is for war. Mr. Weaver, one of Colonel Cooke's guides, said a smoke raised on the mountains was a signal for peace and a token for help, and a smoke raised in a valley was a sign for war. I remember when the Colonel wanted to raise an Indian near the copper mines in Sonora he ordered a smoke to be made on the top of a mountain close by, and he got him.

August 7. This morning four horses and one ox were missing; supposed to have been stolen by Indians. Made about fifteen miles and camped on the river. Road rather bad. Indians were seen following us all day.

August 8. Still continued our course down the river making about fifteen miles.

August 9. After making about fifteen miles we camped again on the river in a short bend. This we called Ox Bow Encampment.

August 10. At two this morning the camp was aroused by the guard saying the horses were crossing the river, leaving the corral which we had made by forming our wagons across the narrow neck or bend of the river. On examining there were no horses missing but when daylight came we found that two horses and a mule were gone. There seemed to be no doubts but Indians had gotten them some way, in spite of the guard notwithstanding; our guard affirmed that they were and had been faithful while on duty and when we came to look after the cattle we found a cow and calf were missing. Ten men were sent out after the animals, when they overtook some Indians and recovered one horse and one mule. One of the men, Mr. Dimond, was shot in the breast by an arrow from an Indian, but it did

119

not prove fatal. After breakfast the calf belonging to the lost cow came up with an arrow sticking in its guts and some of the camp had to knock it in the head.[12]

August 11. Traveled twelve miles and camped. A little dog belonging to one of the company came up, being shot with arrows; it had remained behind in the morning, eating on the remains of the calf.[13]

August 12. Left Carson River. Traveled rather a north-west course for twenty-five miles, when we struck the old Truckee road on the east side of the Truckee River.[14] Here our packers left us and went ahead.

August 13. Laid by.

August 14. After traveling about eight miles over a sandy road, we then had a hard, smooth road and en-camped at the boiling springs, making about twenty-five miles. Here we made our tea and coffee without fire to heat the water. A little dog walked up so near to one of these springs as to lose his balance, fell in, and was instantly scalded to death and boiled to pieces. Here was no water for our stock.

August 15. At eleven last night we rolled out for water. The moon shone bright, and a good road. At six this morning arrived at the sink of the Humboldt and camped. The water here was not very good. Cattle did not like it.

---

12. The Huntington version records that the wounded man, Mr. Diamond, was not a Mormon, and that the calf soon died of its wound.

13. The camp was named Holmes' Hole because of a fine hole of water in the river (Huntington).

14. "The old road that we had been traveling on, at the time we met Sam Brannan and Captain Brown about a year ago" (Huntington). The period from August 9 to the end of the trek can be collated with the Huntington version. The latter is more detailed than Bancroft. Un-der the date of August 15 Bigler speaks at length of Hazen Kimball, who had been a Mormon but had become dissatisfied with the settlement and the people at Salt Lake (See *James Clyman,* p. 287). However, here as in the following entries, the Bancroft version omits nothing of historical interest.

Towards evening eighteen emigrant wagons rolled in and camped by us. They had met our packers about forty miles ahead of us and had traveled about one hundred miles without water. These emigrants had come by way of Fort Hall. There was one family in the crowd by the name of Hazen Kimball that had wintered at the Salt Lake and had moved in March to Fort Hall. Kimball said he did not like the Salt Lake country and had left, but the people there had been sowing wheat all last fall and winter and had put in eight thousand acres of grain. At this camp we lost a cow. She mired and in her struggles broke a blood vessel.

August 16. Made twenty miles. Road good. At this camp the water is a little better and runs a little. The stock looks bad, not having had much grass and water since leaving the Truckee. Today we met twenty-five wagons, emigrants for California.

August 17. We were followed all day by Indians. At night had plenty of good running water. Late in the evening, when we drove up our stock, we found that one of the horses was shot with a poison arrow. Three Indians had just come into camp with their bows and arrows. We showed the wounded horse to them and took their bows from them and gave them to understand that they could not leave camp. They set up a dreadful fuss. One of them shed a heavy shower of tears. Indeed I began to pity him. They pow-wowed over the animal when the one in tears put his mouth over the wound and sucked out all the poison, and the wound healed up and the next morning we gave them their bows and arrows and let them go.

August 18. Some of the cattle began to get lame, and we had to throw them and take the gravel from their feet.

August 19. This morning we had to leave a cow. She had become so tenderfooted that she could not travel. As we were making camp a lot of Indians, men, women and children, took to their heels for life as soon as they saw us roll in sight. Before we had been in camp two hours, we saw two of our horses walking around with arrows sticking in them. Along here there was no grass for the stock, except along on the river in the willows, which offered the redskins an excellent chance to skulk and shoot our animals when they went in among the willows to feed. Our boys sallied out; some of them got sight of an Indian or two and fired at them but with what effect we never knew, perhaps might have scared them a little.

August 20. Laid by.

August 21. Made about twenty-eight miles. Today two horses and a colt were shot with poison arrows. The willows along the river in places affording so good a chance that our stock are shot in broad daylight as we drive along the road, and it appears to me that Indians prefer horse beef to any other meat. It seems that it is their calculation, that, when a horse is shot with a poison arrow, the animal will become so sick that it will be left, and of course will fall into their hands.

August 22. Made an early encampment after making about ten miles. We had to leave one of our wounded horses.

August 23. Left another horse for beef. Made about eighteen or twenty miles.

August 24. Made a short drive.

August 25. This morning a horse was missing, either strayed off or stolen in the night by Indians. Made about eighteen miles and camped. After we had struck camp seven Indians came in camp, appeared very friendly, and promised they would not shoot our horses.

August 26. We met ten wagons of emigrants.

August 27. Laid by. At 3:00 P.M. the camp came together at Addison Pratt's tent and held prayer meeting. Just as the meeting was over, Captain S. Hensley and a company of ten on packs came up.[15] We were informed by Captain Hensley that it was not more than three hundred and eighty miles to Salt Lake by taking a certain route that he had found and had just come. He gave us a way bill saying the route was a good one and easy to be found, saving at least eight or ten days travel as it was our intention to go by way of Fort Hall. Mr. Hensley had gotten defeated in attempting to take Hastings' Cutoff and had turned back; by so doing discovered this new route and found it to be much nearer than Hastings'.

X.

THE END OF
THE TREK: 1848

On the thirtieth we met Captain Chiles [1] and Company of forty-eight wagons: emigrants. He gave us a way bill

15. Samuel P. Hensley, a prominent Californian in Sutter's employment, had gone to Washington, D. C., in 1847 and was on his return trip. See Morgan in *Utah Historical Quarterly,* XIX, 249 f.; *James Clyman* pp. 290 f.

Camp, in Appendix F of *James Clyman,* prints some fragmentary entries between August 15 and 31, which were taken from the Day Book.

1. Joseph B. Chiles, a pioneer in California since 1841 had gone east with Commodore Stockton in 1847, like Hensley, and returned now, leading a large party including his family. Bigler's diary does not describe the Chiles cutoff. According to Korns (*Utah Historical Quarterly,* XIX, 251) it was the route of 1841 which Chiles had traveled in company with some of the great California pioneers: Bartelson, Bidwell, Weber. Obviously the Mormons did not know that this time Chiles had come via Fort Hall. Otherwise they would not have sent out scouts on the fifth and the eighth to find the tracks of Chiles's trail.

purporting to give a still nearer route than that of Hensly. We bought of Captain Chiles's Company some bacon and buffalo meat.[2]

September 1.[3] Made sixteen miles, when in the afternoon it became cold and the wind blew briskly from the northwest; about sundown it rained.

September 2. Rained and snowed and became very disagreeable. Made a few miles and camped.

September 3. Cleared up in the night, and this morning it was very cold. The tops of the mountains were capped with the late snow, while here in the valley is a heavy frost and everything frozen hard. As our campground was not very good we concluded to roll out until we found a more suitable place and lay over a day, and we went about twenty miles before we found it. Here several of the natives came in camp to trade dressed buckskins for knives, clothing; some of them had rifles and wanted to trade for powder.

September 4. Laid by and killed a beef, while some went a-fishing and caught a fine lot of what some of the boys called salmon trout.

September 5. Cool and frosty. About eight we rolled out; went about two miles and found that one horse and a mule were missing. It was then concluded to camp here and hunt up the animals and at the same time send four pioneers ahead to find where we were to leave the road to take Captain Chiles's cutoff and meet us the day after to-

---

2. According to Day Book and the Huntington version, they had met the Chiles party on the preceding day.

3. The Day Book has this entry for August 31: "We had plenty of dust today; made about 10 miles and went into camp early as there was plenty of good grass and water. Here Hastings Cutoff leaves the main road to our right, leading towards a low gap or notch in the mountain some 15 or 20 miles off."

morrow. In the evening the boys that went to hunt for the horse and mule returned with them. The mule however was shot through the thigh by Indians. Lieutenant Thompson lost a horse eating or drinking something that gave him the scours.

September 6. Made about twenty miles when we found a note left by our four men to camp here. Today several sage hens were killed.

September 7. After making about ten miles we met our four pioneers at the head of the Humboldt. Here we camped and had a report from them which, according to Mr. Chiles's map or way bill, must be the place to turn off; but they had been ten miles or more ahead and found no trace where Captain Chiles had been. Neither had they found water, and two of them got sick and of course turned back to meet the camp. That evening the camp came together to talk the thing over and consider whether it was best to continue this new route or go Hensley's. It was decided not to give up Chiles's route but on the morrow morning send out five men with plenty of water to explore and make a thorough hunt for Captain Chiles's trail. Our [camp] was to follow after until they gained the summit at the head of the Humboldt, some five or six miles, where there were several springs, and there await until they heard from the five men or for a smoke that would be raised as a signal for the camp to come ahead. Next morning early, they set out accompanied by one hunter, and the camp hooked on and rolled after them to the top of the mountain to await developments. At sundown four of the men returned. They had found nothing. At eleven in the night the other pioneer and hunter got in. They had been farther south but found no trail where wagons had been or anything else in the shape of white men. Neither had they found water. If they had, our camp would have struck out on that cutoff at all hazards. A meeting was called immediately to get the mind of the camp whether to continue on this cutoff or go the Fort Hall road until we come to Hensley's route and take that. It was soon voted to try the latter if we could find it, which from the chart could easily be done. The next morning we rolled back to the campground we had left the morning previous and camped here within a few rods where the Humboldt River comes out of the ground. We caught lots of trout. The surrounding country looks beautiful with low mountains all around with plenty of grass.[4]

September 10. Made about twenty-four miles and camped in Hot Spring Valley. Six miles back, the running water was hot. A few Indians came in to trade.

September 11. Made fifteen miles.

September 12. Passed over some rough road. Made sixteen miles and camped. Here I caught a fine mess of trout.[5]

September 14. While at breakfast this morning an Indian came in with a mule to swap for a horse. No doubt but the mule was a stolen one from some emigrant. Mr. Brown gave the Indian a trade. Made twelve miles and camped in the mountain. At dusk our pilots that had gone ahead in the morning returned and reported they had found Captain Hensley's cutoff about eight miles ahead.

September 15. Set off this morning in good spirits. Everyone seemed to feel fine, and after making about eight miles we came into a chain of low mountains, and nearby on our left were two towering rocks near each other which

4. This entry summarizes the entries from the seventh to the ninth without omitting anything essential. In the Day Book he still speaks of Mary's River, the trappers' name for the Humboldt before the Frémont-Preuss maps. In the Day Book as well as in the Huntington version he calculates fairly accurately the distance covered: 588 miles.

5. According to the Day Book and the Huntington version they traveled this day down Goose Creek, a tributary of the Snake River.

Mr. A. Pratt named the Twin Sisters.[6] Since known by travelers as the City of Rocks, as there are several masses piled up all round in the same neighborhood. Here we left the Fort Hall Road on our left taking a course directly east through sage brush and over rocks and boulders and camped on Cash Creek [7] making today about thirteen miles.

September 16. Continued down this stream ten miles and camped. We were met by eleven Indians of the Snake nation on horseback.

September 17. Last night one of the guards [Azariah Smith] lost a silver case from off a valuable silver watch belonging to Mr. E. Green. How that was done the guard could not tell and remains to this day a mystery! At this camp we left the Cash [Cassia], it turning and running north, while our course was east over and through sage-brush for ten or twelve miles. Camped on the side of a mountain where there was plenty of cedar timber.[8]

September 19. This morning we could see, as we supposed, Salt Lake off to the southeast of our camp, some twenty or thirty miles. Today we made some twenty miles east and camped on Deep Creek. Here a lot of the natives came in on horseback to trade and [they] will camp with us.

---

6. They were now in the southwest corner of present-day Idaho. Pratt's name is still preserved. The masses of rocks around it are designated as (Silent) City of Rocks on modern topographical maps.

7. Cassia Creek, western fork of Raft River. Spelled Casier in the Day Book and Cashier in the Huntington version. The name is derived from the French *cajeux*, "small raft" (Morgan, *Pritchard* pp. 161 f.). On modern topographical maps this stream is now designated as a branch of the Raft River.

8. Bigler confuses his record by omitting the entry for the 18th and misdating his entries thereafter. He recognized his error in the Day Book, but it persisted in the later versions of his diary. I have consequently corrected his dates, beginning on the 19th, when they traveled north of Salt Lake, approximately following present Highway 30.

September 20. Made about eighteen or twenty miles.

September 22. Lost a cow last night. What became of her we could not tell. Made about twelve miles and camped by a spring of brackish water and poor feed.

September 22. Rained in the night. Made today about eighteen miles and camped on the Malad. Here the boys caught fish almost as fast as they threw their hooks in. We are now in sight of Bear River [9] and the whole camp is all life talking and singing, and tomorrow night the camp has the promise of a new song to be composed for the occasion by Mr. Daniel Denit.

September 23. This morning in crossing the Malad we broke down a wagon. The crossing was very bad. The stream was narrow, not very deep, but the bottom very soft and muddy. In coming out on the opposite side, passing on for six or seven miles we came to Bear River, the fording of which was good. In consequence of breaking down we made but a short drive and camped on the east side of Bear River. Just as we went into camp a shower of rain was upon us, but it soon held up. Almost every man brought in an arm full of wood to have one common fire, around which we were to have some singing. After supper and prayers the camp just enjoyed themselves, singing songs, telling "yarns," cracking jokes on each other, etc.

September 24. Made only a few miles owing to many of our calves being so tenderfooted.

September 25. Today we had the luck to break down three of our wagons. However we reached the first settlement where Ogden City now stands. Here Captain James Brown (of the Mormon Battalion) had bought out one Miles Goodyear, an old mountaineer and trapper, and had

---

9. Malad and Bear rivers run almost parallel here. In the Day Book and the Huntington version the Malad is called Muddy Creek.

formed a settlement with only some half dozen families.[10]

September 26. Had a good road. Made some eighteen miles.

September 27. Laid by. The day was spent in mending wagons, eating roasting ears and melons. Washing clothes, trimming hair, shaving up, and dressing seemed to be the order of the day. Everybody in camp busy and in the finest of spirits, and [it was] said to be only about twenty-five or thirty miles to Great Salt Lake City. Here our company began to scatter or drop off, for a few concluded to stop here at least for a while.

The next morning, however, the majority continued their journey for the main settlement. Made about half the distance and camped on Hates [Haights] Creek.

September 29. We arrived at the great Salt Lake settlement where a city was already laid out and named "Great Salt Lake City." Here I found my sister Emeline and husband John W. Hess, at whose house I made my home. They had come in the season before. I found the people busy in almost every branch of industry, such as working roads in to the canyons, getting out timbers, making adobes, preparing to build houses. A sawmill was already erected and running; others were in course of construction. A flouring mill was nearly completed, owned by Mr. Neff on the Cottonwood eight miles from the city. The first crop was now harvested. Wheat was excellent though a great deal was so short that it had to be pulled up by the roots. Buckwheat was first rate. Where Salt Lake City now stands was almost one grand buckwheat patch. Po-

---

10. Miles Goodyear was probably the first farmer who made things grow before the Mormons arrived. He had built his trading post, Fort Buenaventura on the Weber River, in 1846. See Kelly and Howe, *Miles Goodyear* (Salt Lake City, 1937) and Morgan, "Miles Goodyear and the Founding of Ogden," *Utah Historical Quarterly*, XXI, 195 ff., 307 ff.

tatoes were fine. Corn light and the fodder short. The
mountaineers did not believe that anything would grow
to do much good. So little faith had Mr. Bridger (an old
mountaineer and trapper) that he told some of our people, that he would give a thousand dollars for the first
bushel of corn raised in this valley.[11]

XI.

BIGLER'S LATER
YEARS: 1848-1900

The arrival in Salt Lake City marked the end of Bigler's
career as a historical figure—that is, as a participant in
the great events which shaped our nation and as a chronicler of these events. He was sent once more to California
and twice to Hawaii, and he continued to write, but in general the half century which he still lived was unexciting
and commonplace. There is little of major interest in
what he later wrote, except the three journeys he undertook for the Church.

In Salt Lake City Bigler found a city lot reserved for
him. He bought "dobies" [adobe bricks] and built himself a one-room house, fifteen by seventeen feet. He lived

---

11. The articles which Bigler had bought at Sutter's Fort are listed
at the end of the Huntington version. The provisions which he brought
to Salt Lake City are given at the end of the Utah version. They show
that Bigler's connection with Sutter for a few months brought rich
dividends even though Sutter may not have been able to pay cash for
his services. Bigler in his decent way never mentions Sutter's indebted-
ness to him, while Brown loudly bewails the fact that Sutter did not pay
him in addition to the large bag of gold dust which he brought to Salt
Lake City.

there with his sister Emeline Hess until her husband's return in July, 1849. Since he had brought a fair store of goods and provisions from California he could look forward with confidence to a good start in the new colony. It was not to be.

President Brigham Young, otherwise strongly opposed to hunting for gold, had given John Smith, who was in need of money, the permission to send someone to California to dig gold for him and make his declining years comfortable. Father Smith, who was the uncle of the founder of the Mormon Church, selected Bigler to do this chore for him. With James Keeler, who had also been commissioned to dig gold by Smith's son-in-law, Thomas Callister, Bigler left Salt Lake City on October 12, 1849, and two days later joined the Flake-Rich Company of packers in Provo.[1] They traveled via the Old Spanish Trail and the Cajon Pass and mined with moderate success until September, 1850.

At that time a number of Mormon gold seekers had their headquarters at Slapjack Bar on the Middle Fork of the American River. Here Bigler took up his pen again after seven months of silence. On September 23, 1850, he wrote a pessimistic entry, ending it with the words, "I am tired of mining and of the country and long to be at home among the Saints." In August he had made a gesture of fulfilling his promise by sending one hundred dollars to Mr. Smith—but he had to borrow it.[2]

Hence it is easy to understand their satisfaction when Charles C. Rich, one of the twelve apostles of the Church, appeared in the camp on September 25 and appointed Bigler and eight others of the Mormon miners to missionary duty in the Hawaiian Islands. They all realized that their

1. See Hafen and Hafen, *Journals of Forty-Niners.*
2. Book "B." Copies in the Bancroft and Huntington libraries.

prospecting was not profitable and that they could live cheaper in the Islands than in the mines. They worked until their claim gave out on October 15, and on November 15, 1850, they boarded a British vessel in San Francisco.

In the Islands the Mormons found fertile ground.[3] By October 6, 1853, Bigler could record that the Church had fifty-eight branches on the Islands, twenty-nine elders, seventy-two priests, and many teachers and deacons. Bigler had become president of the Church on Oahu Island, and to make their mission more effective it was decided to have the Book of Mormon and other Church literature printed in the native language. Bigler recorded the content of one of his sermons, which gives an indication of the method used by the missionaries in converting the Hawaiians. On Sunday, July 10, 1853 he enters in his diary: "I preached twice and enjoyed much of the spirit. My subject matter was in regard to the people that their forefathers was a white people highly favored to the Lord, but because of transgression the Lord caused a dark skin and gave them an ignorant heart, but that he had his eye on them to do them good and remove their dark skins and give them an understanding heart."

Bigler remained poor. His "congregration" apparently paid for his daily needs, but for a new pair of shoes or pants he was dependent on the charity of the more well-to-do brethren. In the summer of 1854 he was released from his missionary work and embarked for San Francisco on August 12. Until the spring Bigler had to work as a farmhand to earn the money for the trip home. July

3. The Hawaiian experiences are taken from "Extracts from missionary experiences of Bigler." Copies in the Bancroft and Huntington libraries.

20, 1855 he arrived in Salt Lake City after an absence of almost six years.

He stayed with his father in Farmington until he married Cynthia Jane Whipple, November 18, 1855. With his wife and a cow, 'Lil,' which his father presented to him, he started farming, and in September, 1856, he rented a farm on shares in Farmington. He did not enjoy his family and farm very long. In February of the following year Brigham Young ordered him on another mission to the Hawaiian Islands.

To earn the money for the journey Bigler and his fellow missionary had to drive a herd of six hundred twenty-five head of cattle and conduct eight wagons with ten tons of flour to Carson Valley for distribution in California. They left May 14, traveled via the Humboldt River route and arrived in Stockton July 11. On August 22, 1857, the missionaries left San Francisco on the clipper *John Land.*

This second mission was a complete failure. Bigler was elected president of the Church for the Hawaiian Islands and tried his best to realize the old dream of having a printing press set up to publish Mormon literature in the native language. But the natives had lost the faith instilled in them a few years before, and Bigler "preached to the walls." He had to try to raise money by peddling Church literature to merchants and public houses. Even if Bigler's efforts to reëstablish the Church had been successful, the days of the Mormons on the Islands were numbered. As early as November 20, a letter was received from Brigham Young, advising the elders on the Islands to return to the United States, and when the so-called "Mormon War" of 1857–58 developed the epistles from Brigham Young became mandatory. On May 1, 1858, Bigler and the remaining non-Hawaiian Mormons left for San Francisco.

After working during the summer months for a Mormon farmer to get the funds for the journey home Bigler joined a group of returning Mormons and reached Ogden on October 26, 1858.

The remainder of his life is uneventful. For the third mission to the Hawaiian Islands after 1874, which is mentioned by Norman Burns in the *History of the Bigler Family*, I could find no records. He kept a diary sporadically. But outside of affairs of the family there is little of interest in his records. He managed his farm, taught school for some time in Richville, Morgan County, wrote occasionally for the *Juvenile Instructor* and other journals. In 1875 Brigham Young, remembering Bigler's selfless devotion to the Church, employed him for duties "in the holy ordinance of the Endowment," first in Salt Lake City, then in the temple of St. George. The United States government also remembered his services—beginning in 1887 he received a monthly pension of eight dollars, later raised to twelve.

Although like a good Mormon he believed in polygamy or, as the Saints euphemistically say, celestial marriage, he remained monogamous. After the death of his first spouse in 1874 he married Eleanor Emmett in 1878 and continued to beget children until in his seventies. When one of his daughters in 1897 left to study at the Academy of Provo, he gave her one dollar, the only money he had, and even that had been sent to him by a nephew.

An unexpected honor came to him in 1898. The Society of California Pioneers celebrated the golden anniversary of the discovery of gold from January 22–31, 1898, and thanks to the tireless efforts of John S. Hittell, the four surviving members of Marshall's crew who had been present on that fateful day of January 24, 1848, Henry W. Bigler, Azariah Smith, William Johnson, James S. Brown attended the celebration in San Francisco. The Pioneer Society paid all expenses, and George Q. Cannon of the Church presidency was generous enough to furnish Bigler with a suit of clothes and ten or fifteen dollars of pocket money. For a man of more than modest pretensions the jubilee celebration was something overwhelming, and the recording of his reception in San Francisco is the last lengthy entry he made in his diaries.[4]

In the following year when he was invited to attend the fiftieth anniversary of California statehood in San Jose, he had to decline with thanks. He felt too old "to travel so far from home."

A year later, November 24, 1900, he died.

The only claim of Bigler to a niche in the history of the American West rests on the fact that he became, more or less accidentally, the chronicler of certain events during the decisive years of 1846, 1847, 1848. Most of his journals contribute something new and unique, and the march of the Mormon Battalion, which has been recorded and described in numerous books, receives in his writing a new and individual note. Bigler possessed three qualities which made him a great chronicler: his ability to write in a realistic and unpretentious style, his keen power of observation, his strict adherence to the truth. This, I believe, places the modest and shy farmer's son in the front rank of the chroniclers who have contributed to the history of our great West.

---

4. *Utah Historical Quarterly* V, 145 ff.

BIBLIOGRAPHY

This list contains only publications and manuscripts quoted in this book. Additional occasional references are in the footnotes.

Bailey, Paul D. *Sam Brannan and the California Mormons.* Los Angeles, 1959.

Bancroft, Hubert Howe. *History of California.* San Francisco, 1884–1890. 7 vols.

Bekeart, Philip Baldwin. "James Wilson Marshall, Discoverer of Gold," *Society of California Pioneers Quarterly,* I, No. 3.

Bieber, Ralph P. *Exploring Southwestern Trails, 1846–1854.* Glendale, 1938.

Bliss, Robert S. "The Journal of Robert S. Bliss, with the Mormon Battalion," *Utah Historical Quarterly,* IV, Nos. 3 and 4. *See also* XXVII, No. 4.

Brown, James S. *California Gold.* Oakland, 1894.

[————.] *First Discovery of Gold in California.* Salt Lake City, 1953.

————. *Life of a Pioneer.* Salt Lake City, 1900. Reprinted 1960 under the title *Giant of the Lord.*

Burns, Norman. *The Bigler Family.* Privately printed, 1960.

"California Gold Discovery," *California Historical Society Quarterly,* XXVII, 107–162. Articles by Knowland, Neasham, Heizer, Fenenga.

Caughey, John W. *Gold Is the Cornerstone.* Berkeley and Los Angeles, 1948.

Clyman, James. *James Clyman, Frontiersman.* Edited by Charles L. Camp. Portland, Oregon, 1960.

Cooke, P. St. George. *Journal of the March of the Mormon Battalion.* 30th Congress. Special Session. Senate Document 2.

Coy, Owen C. *Gold Days.* Los Angeles, 1929.

DeVoto, Bernard A. *The Year of Decision, 1846.* Boston, 1943.

Egenhoff, Elisabeth L. *The Elephant as They Saw It.* Supplement, *California Journal of Mines and Geology,* October, 1949.

Emory, W. H. *Notes of a Military Reconnoissance.* 30th Congress. 1st Session. [House] Executive Document 41.

Golder, Frank Alfred. *The March of the Mormon Battalion.* New York, 1928 (Contains Standage's diary.)

Gudde, Erwin G. *Sutter's Own Story.* New York, 1936.

Hafen, LeRoy R. *Journals of Forty-Niners.* Glendale, California, 1954.

Hess, John W. "John W. Hess, with the Mormon Battalion." *Utah Historical Quarterly,* IV, 47 ff.

Hittell, Theodore H. *History of California.* San Francisco, 1897. 4 vols.

Jones, Nathaniel V. "The Journal of Nathaniel V. Jones, with the Mormon Battalion," *Utah Historical Quarterly,* III, 6 ff.

Korns, J. Roderic. *West from Fort Bridger.* Salt Lake City, 1951.

Lee, John D. *Journals of John D. Lee.* Edited by Charles Kelly. Salt Lake City, 1938.

Lienhard, Heinrich. *From St. Louis to Sutters Fort.* Translated and edited by Erwin G. Gudde and Elisabeth K. Gudde. Norman, Oklahoma, 1961.

[Marshall, James] "The Discovery of Gold in California," *Hutchings California Magazine,* November, 1857.

Mason, Richard B. [Report] 31st Congress. 1st Session. House Executive Document 17.

New Helvetia Diary: A Record of Events Kept by John A. Sutter and His Clerks. San Francisco, 1939.

Parsons, George F. *The Life and Adventures of James W. Marshall.* San Francisco, 1935 (New edition).

Patton, Annaleone D. *California Mormons.* Salt Lake City, 1961.

Pritchard, James A. *The Overland Journey of James A. Pritchard . . . 1849.* Edited by Dale L. Morgan. Denver, 1959.

Roberts, B. H. *The Mormon Battalion.* Salt Lake City, 1919.

Scherer, James A. B. *The First Forty-Niner.* New York, 1925.

Scott, Reva. *Samuel Brannan and the Golden Fleece.* New York, 1944.

Smith, Azariah. "Diary." *Overland Monthly,* February, 1888.

Standage, Henry. *See* Golder.

Stanley, Reva H. "Sutter's Mormon Workmen at Natoma and

Coloma in 1848," California Historical Society *Quarterly,* XIV, 269–282.

Stellman, Louis J. *Sam Brannan, Builder of San Francisco.* New York, 1953.

Stewart, George R. *Ordeal by Hunger.* Boston, 1960.

Sutter, Johann August. Personal Reminiscences. Manuscript, Bancroft Library, Berkeley, California.

Tyler, Daniel. *A Concise History of the Mormon Battalion in the Mexican War.* [n.p.] 1881.

Zollinger, James Peter. *Sutter: The Man and His Empire.* New York and London, 1939.

INDEX

Allen, Ezrah H. (trek to Salt Lake), 113, 115, 116
Allen, James (first commander, Mormon Battalion), 16, 17, 19, 22, 23
American River (California), 70, 108, 111, 112, 117, 131
Apache Indians, 29 ff.
Arkansas River, 24

Bailey, Paul D. (historian), 136
Bailey, Thomas A. (historian), 18, 75
Bancroft, Hubert Howe (historian), 1, 10, 16, 82, 93 f., 136
Bancroft Library, 2, 5, 94, 131
Bancroft version (of Bigler's diaries), 2, 24, 41, 42, 64, 65, 84, 106, 109, 116, 120
Bandini, Juan (San Diego), 56
Barger, James (at Sutter's Mill), 85, 95, 99
Barnstable (ship), 52
Bear River (California), 57, 71
Bear River Valley (California?), 62
Bear River (Utah), 128
Bekeart, Philip (historian), 89, 136
Bennett, Charles, 82, 85, 92, 101
Benton, Thomas Hart, Senator, 17
Bent's Fort (on Arkansas River), 24, 25
Big John Spring or Council Grove (on Santa Fe trail), 22
Bigler, Adelbert (son), 5
Bigler, Hannah (grandmother), 8
Bigler, Henry William, 2, 5, 7, 10, 16, 25, 44, 47, 56, 74, 77, 78, 86 ff., 97, 130 ff., 134
Bigler, Jacob (grandfather), 8; (father), 9
Bigler, Mark (emigrant of 1733), 7
Bigler, Rudolf (historian), 8
Bitter Creek (Wyoming), 74
Blake, William P. (Pacific Railroad Survey), 64
Bliss, Robert S., *Journal* (Mormon Battalion), 38, 50, 56, 62, 64, 72, 80, 136
Boggs, Lilburn W. (Governor of Missouri), 12
Boly, Samuel (Mormon Battalion), 19
Brannan, Samuel (Mormon Elder), 55, 56, 58, 69, 74 ff., 101, 106, 108, 110, 120
Branson, Myrtle B., 6
Bridger, James, 130
Brighton (California), 81, 112
Brooklyn (ship), 55, 56, 58, 59, 69
Brooks, Juanita (historian), 3
Browett, Daniel (at Sutter's Fort), 106, 113, 116
Brown, James (Captain, Mormon Battalion, Pueblo detachment), 26, 76, 77, 120, 128
Brown, James S. (at Sutter's Mill), 85, 87, 89, 94 ff., 99, 101, 103, 105, 109, 110; (trek to Salt Lake), 126, 130, 134, 136
Bryant, Edwin, 80
Buena Vista (Mexico), 52
Burns, Norman (historian), 134, 136

Cahuenga (California), 44

Cajon Pass (California), 131

California, 14, 15, 58, 59, 61, 63 ff., 74 ff., 79, 83 ff., 108, 121

California Pioneers, Society of, 3, 4, 84, 87, 88, 134, 135

California Star (Brannan's newspaper), 59, 108, 109

Californians (Spaniards), 44, 50, 52, 63

Callister, Thomas, 131

Camp, Charles L. (historian), 123, 136

Camp Creek (California), 114

Camps of Israel (Iowa), 58

Cannon, George Q., 135

Cape Horn, 16, 17, 56, 58, 69

Carson River (Nevada), 118, 120

Carson Valley (California, Nevada), 4

Cassia Creek (Idaho), 127

Caughey, John W. (historian), 94, 136

Cerro Gordo (Mexico), 56

Charbonneau, Jean B. (guide), 27, 29

Chihuahua (Mexico), 28, 39, 54

Chiles, Joseph B., 123, 124

Church Historian (Latter-day Saints), 5

City of Rocks (Idaho), 127

Clift, Robert (Lieutenant, Mormon Battalion), 56

Clyman. See *James Clyman*

Coloma (California), 82 ff., 96, 97, 101, 108, 109, 110

Colorado River, 40, 41, 52

Colton, Philander (Mormon Battalion), 61

Columbia River, 15

Congress (U.S. frigate), 51, 53

Cooke, P. St. George (final commander of Mormon Battalion), 26, 27, 28, 29, 30, 32, 33, 34, 36, 37, 38, 39, 40, 44, 45, 46, 47, 50, 51 f., 53, 54, 55, 119, 136

Cooke's Journal, 42, 51

Coray, William (on trek to Salt Lake), 114

Cosumnes River (California), 69, 112, 113, 114

Cottonwood Creek (Utah), 129

Council Bluffs (Iowa), 2, 15, 16, 62

Council Grove. *See* Big John Spring

Cox, Amos (Mormon Battalion), 32

Cox, Henderson (trek to Salt Lake), 113, 116

Coy, Owen C. (historian), 94, 136

Cunningham, Sally Ann (Bigler's stepmother), 9

Daviess County (Missouri), 11

Davis, Daniel C. (Captain, Mormon Battalion), 61

Day Brook (fragment of Bigler's diaries), 6, 116, 117, 123, 124, 126, 127, 128

Deep Creek (Utah), 127

Delta District (California), 69

Denit, Daniel (trek to Salt Lake), 128

Devils Point (Gila Mountains, Arizona), 40

DeVoto, Bernard A. (historian), 14, 136

Dimond (trek to Salt Lake), 119, 120

Doniphan, Alexander W. (commander of a brigade at Far West; in the Mexican War, commander in New Mexico), 54

Donner Lake (California), 74, 79

Donner Party, 72, 73 f., 79

Dunham, Albert (Mormon Battalion), 54

Dykes, George P. (Lieutenant, Mormon Battalion), 23, 29, 50

Egenhoff, Elisabeth L. (historian), 89, 137

El Brazito (New Mexico), 54

Emmett, Eleanor (Bigler's second wife), 134

Evans, Israel (Mormon Battalion), 54; (at Sutter's Mill), 82, 97, 101, 103, 108

143